NEWMAN ON BEING A CHRISTIAN

NEWMAN
ON BEING
A
CHRISTIAN

Ian Ker

UNIVERSITY OF NOTRE DAME PRESS
NOTRE DAME   LONDON

Library of Congress Cataloging-in-Publication Data

Ker, I. T. (Ian Turnbull)
    Newman on being a Christian / Ian Ker.
    p. cm.
    Includes   extensive   quotations   from
    Newman's writings.
    Includes bibliographical references.
    ISBN 0-268-01468-X
    1. Catholic Church—Doctrines—History—
19th century. 2. Church of England—Doctrines
—History—19th century. 3 Newman, John Henry, 1801–1890. I. Newman, John Henry,
1801–1890. Selections. 1990. II. Title.
BX1747.K47   1990
230'.2—dc20   89-40752

For Barry McCormick

CONTENTS

vii

PREFACE

Not only was John Henry Newman not a systematic theologian, but he never attempted to produce any kind of condensed synthesis of his theology. Nor did he ever try to distill his thought in the form, for example, of an introduction to Christianity or Catholicism. There have been anthologies of his writings which have attempted, more or less expansively, to assemble his essential thinking on the Christian faith by grouping together quotations or selections from the collected works of thirty-six volumes (as well as a few volumes published posthumously). But the present book is the first attempt to synthesize Newman's writings in such a way as to draw the kind of outline of Catholic Christianity such as, it is perhaps permissible to suppose on the basis of his published works, he might have sketched out himself.

Given that most of Newman's publications were written and issued for specific occasions, it is not very surprising that the works do not easily yield anything like a comprehensive outline. To take some obvious examples, there are no separate chapters here on the Trinity or the person of Christ, while the chapter on the sacraments contains no account of the sacrament of marriage. This does not mean that it would have been impossible to collect enough material to fill such gaps, but it does mean that Newman's thought on these subjects was not sufficiently fresh or original or substantial to justify their inclusion on the scale one would normally expect in this kind of book. Conversely, the chapter on the Church may seem comparatively excessive in length; but again this simply reflects Newman's own interests and preoccupations. *Newman on Be-*

ing a Christian, then, is a deliberately and essentially incomplete study to the extent that it does not purport to represent how Newman himself would have treated certain more or less neglected topics had he ever himself written such a book.

This book is intended for three kinds of readers (who may indeed overlap). First, there are those who are looking for a convenient source from which to introduce themselves to or to refresh their understanding of Christianity. The disadvantage of this particular source is clearly its incompleteness and unevenness; but its advantage surely is that it offers an approach to Catholic Christianity through the mind of one of the world's greatest Christian thinkers, who also happens to be one of the great prose stylists of the English language. The second class of readers for whom this book was written are those who wish to learn something, in a practical kind of way, about the thought and spirituality of a man who is now seen as "the Father of the Second Vatican Council" and who is a candidate for formal canonization. Thirdly, there may be readers who are already familiar with the life and work of Cardinal Newman but who would be interested to see the kind of outline of the faith which a synthesis might be able to offer. There is in fact certainly one such reader: the present author, who compiled this book partly for the satisfaction of having a volume that he hopes may be an approximation of the sort of introduction to Christianity that Newman himself might have penned. Certainly, whatever the defects of the present synthesis, Newman would hardly have doubted the value of such a book in this secularized, post-Christian world of today, which he himself predicted with such keen prescience.

I am once again grateful to Mrs. Virginia Lyons for so splendidly transforming an untidy manuscript into an impeccable typescript.

College of St. Thomas   I. T. K.
St. Paul, Minnesota
June, 1989

1

FAITH

Antecedent Probability

Newman first started in his early twenties to think seriously about the problem of faith as a result of one of his younger brothers' abandoning Christian belief. From arguing with his brother, he reached the incisive conclusion that "the rejection of Christianity" rises "from a fault of the heart, not of the intellect," since a "dislike of the contents of Scripture is at the bottom of unbelief." This is why "the most powerful arguments for Christianity do not *convince*, only *silence*; for there is at the bottom that secret antipathy for the doctrines of Christianity, which is quite out of the reach of argument." What is striking about his early approach to unbelief is the emphasis placed on subjective as opposed to objective reasons for belief: already for Newman the question is not so much What are the external grounds for believing? as What are the personal factors that in fact move a person to believe or not to believe?

This kind of consideration immediately raised for him the importance of what he came to call "antecedent probability."

We survey moral and religious subjects through the glass of previous habits; and scarcely two persons use a glass of the same magnifying power. I venture confidently to say, that if the contents of a professed revelation on divine things are to be made the test of its genuineness, *no revelation could* be made us; for scarcely two persons can be got together, who will agree in their antecedent or self-originated ideas of God and his purposes towards man.[1]

In other words, our beliefs depend to a considerable extent on what we think is likely to be true, and this in turn depends on the kind of people we are, and what our principles and values are. Thus, right from the start, Newman's defense of religious belief has a strong moral coloring to it. But the "first principles," as Newman came to call them, which determine what we think and believe are not only moral; they underlie all our beliefs and thoughts: "Resolve to believe nothing, and you must prove your proofs and analyze your elements, sinking further and further . . . till you come to the broad bosom of scepticism."[2] Not only religious convictions rest on first principles, but all our thinking is in this general sense hypothetical, and consistency may demand that skepticism about religion should lead to a much wider skepticism. For "First Principles . . . are the means of proof, and are not themselves proved; they rule, and are not proved; they are sovereign on the one hand, irresponsible on the other: they are absolute monarchs . . . they are to the mind what the circulation of the blood and the various functions of our animal organs are to the body . . . they are, in short, the man."[3] Newman's refusal to separate thinking about religion from other kinds of thinking characterized his whole approach to the question of faith.

In the first of a series of university sermons delivered in the Church of St. Mary the Virgin at Oxford between 1839 and 1841, "Faith and Reason, Contrasted as Habits of Mind," Newman protests against the popular idea that faith follows reason as a kind of "moral quality," or, in other words, that having made up our mind what to believe, we then "proceed to adore and to obey" ("Faith follows or not, according to the state of the heart"). On this view, faith ceases to be an intellectual act and becomes a kind of spiritual consequent of reasoning. But, Newman argues, just as a judge "does not make men honest, but acquits and vindicates them," so "Reason need not be the origin of Faith, as Faith exists in the very persons believing, though it does test and verify it." Newman makes a distinction between "a critical" and "a creative power." We may, for example, give reasons for our actions by analyzing our motives, but the reasons are different from the motives. There is certainly no doubt that the New Testament sees "Faith . . . as an instrument of Knowledge and action, unknown to the world before . . . independent of what is commonly understood by Reason." If faith were "merely . . . a believing upon evidence, or a sort of conclusion upon a process of reasoning," then it would scarcely be "a novel principle of action," as the Bible regards it. Just as conscience does not "depend . . . upon some previous processes of Reason" (although it is not "against Reason"), similarly "a child or uneducated person may . . . savingly act on Faith, without being able to produce reasons why he so acts." For faith is "mainly swayed by antecedent considerations," while reason calls for "direct any definite proof."

Religious faith, Newman maintains, is, like all beliefs, "influenced . . . less by evidence, more by previously-entertained principles, views, and wishes," in other words, by "antecedent probabilities." It is when these "prepossessions" are right, that "we are right in believing," albeit "upon slender evidence." Faith, then, is a "moral principle" in the sense that it is "created in the mind, not so much by facts, as by probabilities," which vary according to one's "moral temperament"—"A good man and a bad man will think very different things probable." This is why "a man *is* responsible for his faith, because he is responsible for his likings and dislikings, his hopes and his opinions, on all of which his faith depends." It is those "feelings"—which, Newman carefully adds, "come only of supernatural grace"—that "make us think evidence sufficient, which falls short of a proof in itself." And so it is that "religious minds embrace the Gospel mainly on the great antecedent probability of a Revelation, and the suitableness of the Gospel to their needs." However, not only are "Evidences . . . thrown away" on "men of irreligious minds," but too much emphasis on "arguments from facts" encourages people "to think that Faith is mainly the result of argu-

ment" and that "religious Truth is a legitimate matter of disputa-
tion" without any "preparation of heart": for "the ways towards
Truth are considered high roads open to all men, however
disposed, at all times," on the assumption that "Truth is to be
approached without homage." With the careful balance that
is so characteristic of his thought, Newman proceeds to dismiss
the other extreme, the "wild" anti-intellectual

> notion that actually no proof at all is implied in the maintenance,
> or may be exacted for the profession of Christianity. I would only
> maintain that that proof need not be the subject of analysis, or
> take a methodical form, or be complete and symmetrical, in the
> believing mind; and that probability is its life. I do but say that
> it is antecedent probability that gives meaning to those arguments
> from facts which are commonly called the Evidences of Revela-
> tion; that, whereas mere probability proves nothing, mere facts
> persuade no one; that probability is to fact, as the soul to the body;
> that mere presumptions may have no force, but that mere facts
> have no warmth. A mutilated and defective evidence suffices for
> persuasion where the heart is alive; but dead evidences, however
> perfect, can but create a dead faith.[4]

In the next sermon, "The Nature of Faith in Relation to
Reason," Newman changes his strategy. Refusing now to accept the limited sense in which empiricists like Locke use the
word *reason*, he effectively widens the terms of the debate by
defining faith as "the reasoning of a religious mind, or of what
Scripture calls a right or renewed heart, which acts upon
presumptions rather than evidence; which speculates and ven-
tures on the future when it cannot make sure of it." If faith
is regarded merely as "bad" reason, this is precisely "because it
rests on presumption more, and on evidence less." There is no
doubt that an act of faith is "an exercise of Reason," insofar
as it is "an acceptance of things as real, which the senses do
not convey, upon certain previous grounds." As such, it "is not
the only exercise of Reason, which, when critically examined,
would be called unreasonable, and yet is not so." The "pursuit
of truth" is not exclusively "a syllogistic process," while "the ex-

perience of life contains abundant evidence that in practical matters, when their minds are really roused, men commonly are not bad reasoners," if only because "the principles which they profess guide them unerringly to their legitimate issues." Certainly people "may argue badly, but they reason well; that is, their professed grounds are no sufficient measures of their real ones," which "they do not, or cannot produce, or if they could, yet could not prove to be true, on latent or antecedent grounds which they take for granted." However "full" and "precise" the "grounds" and "however systematic our method, however clear and tangible our evidence, yet when our argument is traced down to its simple elements, there must ever be something assumed ultimately which is incapable of proof."

Faith, then, is not essentially different from other kinds of intellectual activity where "we must assume something to prove anything, and can gain nothing without a venture." In fact, the more important the knowledge is, the more subtle is "the evidence on which it is received," for "we are so constituted, that if we insist upon being as sure as is conceivable, in every step of our course, we must be content to creep along the ground, and can never soar." And so just as "Reason, with its great conclusions, is confessedly a higher instrument than Sense with its secure premises, so Faith rises above Reason, in its subject-matter, more than it falls below it in the obscurity of its process." Like "the most remarkable victories of genius," the act of faith involves "grounds of inference" which "cannot be exhibited," so that the "act of mind" of an uneducated believer "may be analogous to the exercise of sagacity in a great statesman or general, supernatural grace doing for the uncultivated reason what genius does for them."[5]

In "Love the Safeguard of Faith against Superstition," like the previous two sermons preached in 1839, Newman explains that the "antecedent probabilities" on which faith depends are "grounds which do not reach so far as to touch precisely the desired conclusion, though they tend towards it, and may come very near it." An "active," "personal and living" faith is created by "anticipations and presumptions" that "are the creation of the mind itself," and is an acceptance of an "external religion" which "elicits into shape, and supplies the spontaneous desires and presentiments of their minds." The "evidence" for Christianity "tells a certain way, yet might be more," and somebody will believe or not believe "according to . . . the state of his heart." Furthermore, "the antecedent judgment, with which a man approaches the subject of religion, not only acts as a bearing this way or that,—as causing him to go out to meet the evidence in a greater or less degree, and nothing more,—but, further, it practically colours the evidence." This is indeed how "judgments are commonly formed concerning facts alleged or reported in political and social matters, and for the same reason, because it cannot be helped." Unbelief for its part "criticizes the evidence of Religion, only because it does not like it, and really goes upon presumptions and prejudices as much as Faith does, only presumptions of an opposite nature."

Newman allows that "some safeguard of Faith is needed, some corrective principle which will secure it from running (as it were) to seed, and becoming superstition or fanaticism." What, therefore, "gives . . . birth" to faith is also what "disciplines it"—namely, "a right state of heart." In short, "We *believe*, because we *love*." Thus it is the "divinely-enlightened mind" which "sees in Christ the very Object whom it desires to love and worship,— the Object correlative of its own affections." There is, then, a moral as well as an intellectual element in faith:

> Right faith is the faith of a right mind. Faith is an intellectual act; right Faith is an intellectual act, done in a certain moral disposition. Faith is an act of Reason, viz. a reasoning upon presumptions; right Faith is a reasoning upon holy, devout, and enlightened presumptions. Faith ventures and hazards; right Faith ventures and hazards deliberately, seriously, soberly, piously, and humbly, counting the cost and delighting in the sacrifice.

Even though faith "is itself an intellectual act," still "it takes its character from the moral state of the agent" and "is perfected, not by intellectual cultivation, but by obedience."[6]

The eighteenth century, the Age of Reason, had emphasized

the *evidences* for Christianity. But unlike so many of his contemporaries in the nineteenth century, Newman did not react
by adopting a Romantic religion of feelings and imagination.
Rather than opposing faith and reason, Newman redefines faith
in terms of a wider concept of reasoning than had been cur-
rent since the seventeenth century. Concerned with the whole
mind, not just the narrowly logical faculty, he is also anxious
to integrate the intellectual with the moral dimension. But he
remains insistent on the importance of the explicitly and
specifically rational element, as the next sermon, "Implicit and
Explicit Reason," preached in 1840, shows.

> Nothing would be more theoretical and unreal than to suppose
> that true Faith cannot exist except when moulded upon a Creed,
> and based upon Evidence; yet nothing would indicate a more
> shallow philosophy than to say that it ought carefully to be dis-
> joined from dogmatic and argumentative statements. To assert the
> latter is to discard the science of theology from the service of
> Religion; to assert the former, is to maintain that every child, every
> peasant, must be a theologian. Faith cannot exist without grounds
> or without an object; but it does not follow that all who have faith
> should recognize, and should be able to state what they believe,
> and why.

Scripture, Newman argues, makes it clear that faith is sometimes
"attended by a conscious exercise of Reason," but sometimes
is "independent not of objects or grounds (for that is impossible,) but of perceptible, recognized, producible objects and
grounds."

The difference between "the more simple faculties and opera-
tions of the mind, and that process of analyzing and describing
them, which takes place upon reflection," is the difference between implicit and explicit reasoning. The corollary is that faith,
"though in all cases a reasonable process, is not necessarily
founded on investigation, argument, or proof; these processes
being but the explicit form which the reasoning takes in the
case of particular minds." But "no analysis is subtle and delicate
enough to represent adequately the state of mind under which

we believe, or the subjects of belief, as they are presented to our thoughts." It is only to be expected that apologists for Christianity should propose "as reasons for belief" those "secondary points" which "best admit of being exhibited in argument"— that is, the so-called evidences—as opposed to the "more recondite feelings" which are generally "the real reasons" for faith; for it is these latter "momentous reasons" that are not easily open to analysis and demonstration. Even the evidences usually convince only "upon a number of very minute circumstances together, which the mind is quite unable to count up and methodize in an argumentative form." He concludes the sermon on a note of caution: the "argumentative forms" which analyze or test reasoning are "critical, not creative," with the consequence that they are "useful in raising objections, and in ministering to scepticism." Indeed, there is always the danger of "weakening the springs of action by inquiring into them."[7]

The Cumulation of Probabilities

Newman thought that the most "original" idea in the *Oxford University Sermons* (1843) was the argument that "antecedent probability is the great instrument of conviction in religious (nay in all) matters." He later wrote: "It is how you convert factory girls as well as philosophers."[8] Emphasis on probability was an important element in the philosophy of Bishop Joseph Butler (1692–1752), whose classic work *The Analogy of Religion* (1736) had a deeply formative influence on Newman. The problem with this approach, which Newman later found in an amended version in John Keble's writings, was that it tended to undermine the whole idea of certainty. As Newman explained in the *Apologia* (1864), he tried to "complete" the theory by arguing that "absolute certitude . . . was the result of an *assemblage* of concurring and converging probabilities" and that "probabilities which did not reach to logical certainty, might suffice for a mental certitude; that the certitude thus brought about might equal in measure and strength the certitude which was created by the strictest scientific demonstration."[9]

So, for example, in the *Essay on the Development of Christian Doctrine* (1845) Newman talks of a "collection of weak evidences" which "makes up a strong evidence" and of "a converging evidence" which amounts to "proof." And without using the actual term *illative sense*, which does not appear before the *Grammar of Assent* (1870), he refers to the "prudence" or "prudent judgment" which decides when there is enough probability for conviction.[10] A year later, after his entry into the Roman Catholic Church, he insisted that "the measure of probability necessary for certainty" must vary "with the individual mind."[11] On the other hand, his subsequent stay in Rome (1846–47) and his contacts with Roman theologians made him very sensitive to the Church's insistence on "a rational faith . . . built upon right reason." He therefore suggested that reasonable faith could "be the result of converging probabilities, and a cumulative proof" from "cumulating probabilities."[12] He continued to develop this position. The "proof of Religion," he wrote in a letter in 1861, using a striking analogy, "I liken . . . to the mechanism of some triumph of skill . . . where all display is carefully avoided, and the weight is ingeniously thrown in a variety of directions, upon supports which are distinct from, or independent of each other."[13] Or, as he later explained by an even more compelling analogy, "The best illustration . . . is that of a *cable* which is made up of a number of separate threads, each feeble, yet together as sufficient as an iron rod," which "represents mathematical or strict demonstration."[14] The cable will certainly break if enough threads give way, but if the threads hold then the cable is as strong as any metal bar. For, to use yet another image, a cumulation of probabilities is like a "bundle of sticks, each of which . . . you could snap in two, if taken separately from the rest."[15]

"It is," Newman argues in the *Grammar of Assent*, by "the cumulation of probabilities, independent of each other, arising out of the nature and circumstances of the particular case . . . probabilities too fine to avail separately, too subtle and circuitous to be convertible into syllogisms, too numerous and

various for such conversion, even were they convertible," that
"we are enabled to become certain" in matters such as religious
faith which do not pertain to logical demonstration. Newman
emphasizes the rationality of this kind of reasoning ("informal
inference," as he now calls it), which, "does not supersede the
logical form of inference, but is one and the same with it; only
it is no longer an abstraction, but carried out into the realities
of life, its premisses being instinct with the substance and the
momentum of that mass of probabilities, which, acting upon
each other in correction and confirmation, carry it home
definitely to the individual case, which is its original scope."
But in this sort of "implicit" reasoning, the human mind is "unequal to a complete analysis of the motives which carry it on
to a particular conclusion," for it "is swayed and determined
by a body of proof, which it recognizes only as a body, and not
in its constituent parts." Because in this type of "concrete" inference, the "cumulation of probabilities, over and above their
implicit character, will vary both in their number and their
separate estimated value, according to the particular intellect
which is employed upon it," it "follows that what to one intellect is a proof is not so to another, and that the certainty
of a proposition does properly consist in the certitude of the
mind which contemplates it."[16]

    Take, for example, the certainty I have that one day I shall
die. It is obviously impossible to demonstrate a future event
which has not yet taken place, nor is it susceptible to logical
proof. "But what logic cannot do, my own living personal reasoning, my good sense, which is the healthy condition of such personal reasoning, but which cannot adequately express itself in
words, does for me, and I am possessed with the most precise,
absolute, masterful certitude of my dying some day or other."
The fact is, says Newman, that not only our religious beliefs
but also "many of our most obstinate and most reasonable cer-
titudes depend on proofs which are informal and personal, which
baffle our powers of analysis, and cannot be brought under logical
rule, because they cannot be submitted to logical statistics."
    It is not surprising, then, that "an intellectual question may

strike two minds very differently, may awaken in them distinct associations, may be invested by them in contrary characteristics, and lead them to opposite conclusions." For in what Newman calls "concrete reasonings," we "judge for ourselves, by our own lights, and on our own principles; and our criterion of truth is not so much the manipulation of propositions, as the intellectual and moral character of the person maintaining them." In other words, because a person's beliefs are personal, ultimately they will depend on what kind of a person he or she is. This does not mean that all beliefs are merely relative and subjective; it is rather the case

> that truth there is, and attainable it is, but that its rays stream in upon us through the medium of our moral as well as our intellectual being; and that in consequence that perception of its first principles which is natural to us is enfeebled, obstructed, perverted, by allurements of sense and the supremacy of self, and, on the other hand, quickened by aspirations after the supernatural; so that at length two characters of mind are brought out into shape, and two standards and systems of thought,—each logical, when analyzed, yet contradictory of each other, and only not antagonistic because they have no common ground on which they can conflict.[17]

Because the first principles that are most relevant to religious belief are moral ones, a good person is more likely to be a believer than a bad person. For to "attempt to *see*" these first principles "by means of the intellect" rather than by the conscience was, Newman thought, similar to the mistake of "attempting by the intellect to see the physical facts" which are perceived by the senses, which in turn "*enable* the intellect to act, by giving it something to act upon."[18] The modern insistence on simply using the intellect in religious inquiry was, he believed, analogous to the medieval Schoolmen's use of syllogistic reasoning instead of empirical observation in scientific investigation. In fact, of course, Newman thought that the unbeliever refuses to believe not on so-called rational grounds but ultimately because of different first principles which lead as inexorably to unbelief as the moral first principles of the believer lead to faith.

In faith, then, and in all the important beliefs in life that we cannot prove, Newman holds that "that supra-logical judgment, which is the warrant for our certitude about them, is not mere common-sense, but the true healthy action of our ratiocinative powers, an action more subtle and more comprehensive than the mere appreciation of a syllogistic argument." This is why "a proof, except in abstract demonstration, has always in it, more or less, an element of the personal, because 'prudence' is not a constituent part of our nature, but a personal endowment." We become certain "by the action of our own minds, by our own individual perception of the truth in question, under a sense of duty to those conclusions and with an intellectual conscientiousness." In this kind of nonlogical thinking, where personality is such an important factor,

> the conclusion . . . is foreseen and predicted rather than actually attained; foreseen in the number and direction of accumulated premises, which all converge to it, and as the result of their combination, approach it more nearly than any assignable difference, yet do not touch it logically (though only not touching it,) on account of the nature of its subject-matter, and the delicate and implicit character of at least part of the reasonings on which it depends.

And so "it is that the practised and experienced mind is able to make a sure divination that a conclusion is inevitable, of which his lines of reasoning do not actually put him in possession."[19]

It is not, therefore, "skill in argumentation" as much as "judgment" which is the key to attaining to truth in nonlogical subjects. And this intellectual judgment, when it is functioning properly, Newman calls the "illative sense." Where logical proof is not available, there is no other "warrant" we can appeal to in order to justify our being certain apart from that "sole and final judgment" which "is committed to the personal action of the ratiocinative faculty, the perfection of which I have called the Illative Sense." While rejecting skepticism, Newman readily admits that he can see "no ultimate test of truth besides the

testimony born to truth by the mind itself." The judgment of
one's own mind, that is, the illative sense, has to decide "the
limit of converging probabilities and the reasons sufficient for
a proof." The illative sense is also concerned with first principles, "which in all reasoning are assumptions . . . very often
of a personal character, which are half the battle in the inference
with which the reasoning is to terminate." These include "the
aspects in which a question is to be viewed," "the principles
on which it is to be considered," and "the arguments by which
it is decided."[20]

While accepting that there are "grounds intrinsically and objectively and abstractedly demonstrative" to prove Christianity, Newman argues that such arguments are not necessarily
irresistible, as is shown by the fact that people are not in practice persuaded by them. For it is impossible to "convert" people
without their sharing certain "assumptions," since "without
assumptions no one can prove anything about anything."
Because, therefore, "scientific demonstrations" are not the way
people come to faith, he asserts that "it is more congenial to
my own judgment to attempt to prove Christianity in the same
informal way in which I can prove for certain that I have been
born into this world, and that I shall die out of it." But again,
"if any one starts from any other principles but ours, I have
not the power to change his principles, or the conclusion which
he draws from them, any more than I can make a crooked man
straight." A person may not be responsible for being "mentally
crooked," but that person will not be convinced of the truth
of Christianity.[21]

The last chapter of the *Grammar of Assent* is in effect an
apologetic essay for Christianity. Newman maintains that belief
in revealed religion depends on belief in natural religion, and
this in turn depends on our listening to the voice of conscience
from which we receive our first intimations of God. All religion
"is founded in one way or other on the sense of sin." Where
there is no sense of guilt, where conscience is replaced by a
mere moral sense, there will be no true religion. But where there
is a consciousness "on the one hand, of the infinite goodness

of God, and, on the other, of our own extreme misery and need," there will also be an anticipation that a revelation has been or will be given. If somebody, then, "has longed for a revelation to enlighten him and to cleanse his heart, why may he not use, in his inquiries after it, that just and reasonable anticipation of its probability, which such longing has opened the way to his entertaining?"

Not only is religion, however, founded on a sense of sin, but our own search for faith must be "conducted under a deep sense of responsibility." Given the reasonableness of a revelation, Newman argues, "There is only one Religion in the world which tends to fulfil the aspirations, needs, and foreshadowings of natural faith and devotion. . . . It alone has a definite message addressed to all mankind." It is Christ "who fulfils the one great need of human nature, the Healer of its wounds, the Physician of the soul." In this fundamental sense Christianity is the final revelation: "Natural Religion is based upon the sense of sin; it recognizes the disease, but it cannot find, it does but look out for the remedy. That remedy, both for guilt and for moral impotence, is found in the central doctrine of Revelation, the mediation of Christ." Christianity alone has "that gift of staunching and healing the one deep wound of human nature."[22]

Newman's approach to the problem of faith was not to deny or to repudiate the traditional arguments for the existence of God and the truth of Christianity, but rather to concentrate on the real considerations and reasons that lie behind the faith of most people, as opposed to the formal grounds traditionally advanced by philosophers of religion. The same was true of his treatment of unbelief: he was not convinced that the unbeliever usually fails or refuses to believe for the reasons traditionally advanced by atheistic philosophers. But Newman was not content simply to describe the dynamics of faith; he also wanted to show that the usual ways in which people come to believe or the reasons they have for believing are perfectly reasonable, even if not strictly *rational* in the narrow sense in which that word has come to be used since the Enlightenment. Probably his most radical challenge to rationalistic ways of thinking was

his insistence on the impossibility of divorcing the moral element from reason in this larger sense, and therefore from faith.
The road to faith, he reiterated in his preaching, is to follow
one's conscience and to try to live a Christian life: for "the Christian revelation addresses itself to our hearts, to our love of truth
and goodness, our fear of sinning, and our desire to gain God's
favour"; whereas on the other hand, he remarked with almost
brutal frankness, someone "who loves sin does not wish the
Gospel to be true, and therefore is not a fair judge of it."[23]

2

REVELATION

Paganism, Natural Religion, and Conscience

In the *Apologia* Newman tells us how deeply influenced he
was by the philosophy and theology of the early Alexandrian
Church. One aspect of the teaching which he eagerly imbibed
concerned the possibility of revelation outside Judaeo-
Christianity. He learned that

> pagan literature, philosophy, and mythology, properly understood,
> were but a preparation for the Gospel. The Greek poets and sages
> were in a certain sense prophets . . . . There had been a direct-
> ly divine dispensation granted to the Jews; but there had been in
> some sense a dispensation carried on in favour of the Gentiles.
> He who had taken the seed of Jacob for His elect people had not
> therefore cast the rest of mankind out of His sight.[1]

Newman's early reading of the Fathers led to his writing his
first book, *The Arians of the Fourth Century* (1833), in which
he enthusiastically endorsed the Alexandrian doctrine that all
genuine religion comes from God—"There never was a time
when God had not spoken to man, and told him to a certain
extent his duty." It was true that "the Church of God ever has
had, and the rest of mankind never have had, authoritative
documents of truth, and appointed channels of communication
with Him . . . but all men have had more or less the guidance

17

of Tradition, in addition to those internal notions of right and wrong which the Spirit has put into the heart of each individual." Newman calls this "vague and uncertain family of religious truths, originally from God, but sojourning without the sanction of miracle, or a definite home, as pilgrims up and down the world, and discernible and separable from the corrupt legends with which they are mixed . . . the *Dispensation of Paganism*." Arguing that examples of this kind of revelation are to be found in the Old Testament (in the figures, for example, of Job and Balaam), he claims that "there is nothing unreasonable in the notion, that there may have been heathen poets and sages, or sibyls again, in a certain sense divinely illuminated, and organs through whom religious and moral truth was conveyed."[2]

The idea of revelation apart from Christianity was a startling one for Newman's contemporaries, whether Protestant or Catholic. Catholics generally interpreted the dictum "no salvation outside the Church" in a highly literal and exclusive way. And not until the Second Vatican Council did it come to be generally accepted that while indeed there can be no salvation apart from Christ and his Church, all who are saved need not be aware of the means to salvation. According to the council, because people who follow their consciences are in a real sense following Christ, even without knowing it, they are saved through his grace and also to some extent participate in his Church in a hidden way. Again, the council's implicit acknowledgment of the truth in non-Christian religions is anticipated in Newman's practical conclusion that the Christian apologist or missionary should "after St. Paul's manner, seek some points in the existing superstitions as the basis of his own instructions, instead of indiscriminately condemning and discarding the whole assemblage of heathen opinions and practices," thus "recovering and purifying, rather than reversing the essential principles of their belief."[3] Such a strategy in Newman's view is appropriate when one considers that Christianity itself has in fact borrowed elements from other philosophies and religions. It is not only that a "great portion of what is generally received as Christian truth, is in its rudiments or in its separate parts to be found in heathen philosophies and religions," but Scripture shows

> that from the beginning the Moral Governor of the world has scattered the seeds of truth far and wide over its extent; that these have variously taken root, and grown up as in the wilderness, wild plants indeed but living; and hence that, as the inferior animals have tokens of an immaterial principle in them, yet have not souls, so the philosophies and religions of men have their life in certain true ideas, though they are not directly divine. What man is amid the brute creation, such is the Church among the schools of the world; and as Adam gave names to the animals about him, so has the Church from the first looked round upon the earth, noting and visiting the doctrines she found there . . . claiming to herself what they said rightly, correcting their errors, supplying their defects, completing their beginnings, expanding their surmises, and thus gradually by means of them enlarging the range and refining the sense of her own teaching.[4]

The Christian revelation is unique, but it is still "the completion and supplement of Natural Religion, and of previous revelations."[5] Indeed, it is the continuation of "a primeval tradition which is universal" and which must exist "if there was an Adam, a father of men, in direct communication with his Creator."[6]

For Newman, the most fundamental part of revelation is available to everyone because it is to be found in each individual person who listens to the voice of his or her conscience. Conscience, Newman declares, "is the essential principle and sanction of Religion." This is ultimately why he can say, "No people . . . has been denied a revelation from God, though but a portion of the world has enjoyed an authenticated revelation." But in this early sermon ("The Influence of Natural and Revealed Religion respectively," 1830) Newman does not claim that our conscience reveals to us a *personal* God; he merely says that conscience "implies a relation between the soul and a something exterior," without attempting to offer an "argument for a Governor and Judge, distinct from the moral system itself."[7] Four years

later, however, he says in another sermon that "conscience immediately directs" a person's "thoughts to some Being exterior
to himself . . . for a law implies a lawgiver, and a command
implies a superior."[8] The point is dramatized in Newman's account of the conversion of the heroine in his novel *Callista*
(1856), who recognizes in the dictate of her conscience not "a
mere law of my nature," but "the echo of a voice speaking to
me. . . . An echo implies a voice; a voice a speaker. That person I love and I fear."[9] The most fully developed argument from
conscience to a personal God is found in the *Grammar of Assent*, where conscience not only tells us that there is a personal
God but also tells us about him:

> From the perceptive power which identifies the intimations of con-
> science with the reverberations or echoes (so to say) of an exter-
> nal admonition, we proceed on to the notion of a Supreme Ruler
> and Judge, and then again we image Him and His attributes in
> those recurring intimations, out of which, as mental phenomena,
> our recognition of His existence was originally gained.

By discovering God, then, in and through our conscience, we
also discover who He is: "the phenomena of Conscience, as a
dictate, avail to impress the imagination with the picture of
a Supreme Governor, a Judge, holy, just, powerful, all-seeing,
retributive." For conscience "teaches us, not only that God is,
but what He is; it provides for the mind a real image of Him."
There is no doubt in Newman's mind what the most promi-
nent aspect of this image is, although he allows for other aspects
too:

> Now Conscience suggests to us many things about that Master,
> whom by means of it we perceive, but its most prominent teaching,
> and its cardinal and distinguishing truth, is that he is our Judge.
> In consequence, the special Attribute under which it brings Him
> before us, to which it subordinates all other Attributes, is that of
> justice—retributive justice.[10]

The Personal and the Propositional

This highly personalistic approach to revelation is typical of Newman's thought and also characterizes his treatment of God's definitive and final self-revelation in Christ. Here Newman anticipates modern theologians who emphasize that God reveals his own self rather than truths about himself. Thus the revelation of God in Christ is primarily a personal one: "What Catholics, what Church doctors, as well as Apostles, have ever lived on, is not any number of theological canons or decrees, but . . . the Christ Himself, as He is represented in concrete existence in the Gospels."[11] What Newman says of Catholic practice agrees with his own approach as an Anglican:

> As God is one, so the impression which He gives us of Himself is one; it is not a thing of parts; it is not a system. . . . It is the vision of an object. When we pray, we pray, not to an assemblage of notions, or to a creed, but to One Individual Being; and when we speak of Him we speak of a Person. . . . This being the case, all our attempts to delineate our impression of Him go to bring out one idea, not two or three or four; not a philosophy, but an individual idea in its separate aspects.

Our experience of God revealed in Christ is not, of course, an immediate one as it was for the apostles, but is mediated to us through their unique experience of the reality: "The ideas which we are granted of Divine Objects under the Gospel, from the nature of the case and because they are ideas, answer to the Originals so far as this, that they are whole, indivisible, substantial, and may be called real, as being images of what is real."[12]

But if it is true that Newman's theology of revelation was fundamentally personalistic rather than propositional, this does not mean that he was in any way antidogmatic. First of all, although revelation is above all the revelation of a person, this does not imply that it is merely subjective in a vague kind of way. After all, a person speaks, and "Why should God speak, unless He meant to say something? Why should He say it, unless

He meant us to hear?" If there has been a definitive revelation, then "there must be some essential doctrine proposed by it to our faith." In other words, "Religion cannot but be dogmatic; it ever has been."[13] Newman is clear that if revelation is a "vision," it is also a "message."[14] For the gospel "is no mere philosophy thrown upon the world at large, no mere quality of mind and thought, no mere beautiful and deep sentiment or subjective opinion, but a substantive message from above."[15]

The balance that Newman keeps between the personal and the propositional aspects of revelation extends also to his treatment of dogma. In *The Arians of the Fourth Century*, he took a distinctly negative line. Far from dogmatic formulations being desirable for their own sake, he insists there that "freedom from symbols and articles is abstractedly the highest state of Christian communion, and the peculiar privilege of the primitive Church," for "technicality and formalism are, in their degree, inevitable results of public confessions of faith," and "when confessions do not exist, the mysteries of divine truth, instead of being exposed to the gaze of the profane and uninstructed, are kept hidden in the bosom of the Church, far more faithfully than is otherwise possible." However, Newman recognizes that dogmatic definitions are both inevitable and necessary, although "the rulers of the [early] Church were dilatory in applying a remedy, which nevertheless the circumstances of the time imperatively required. They were loath to confess, that the Church had grown too old to enjoy the free, unsuspicious teaching with which her childhood was blest."[16]

Newman's lack of enthusiasm for dogmatic propositions partly resulted from his awareness of the inadequacy of human language to express revelation, which in turn came from his discovery of the early Church's principle of *economy*. His study of the Alexandrian Church introduced him to the theology of Clement and Origen, which was "based on the mystical or sacramental principle, and spoke of the various Economies or Dispensations of the Eternal." Accordingly, the Church's "mysteries are but the expressions in human language of truths to which the human mind is unequal."[17] The principle of economy meant that the doctrine of the Trinity, for example, can be seen only as "the shadow, projected for the contemplation of the intellect, of the Object of scripturally-informed piety: a representation, economical; necessarily imperfect, as being exhibited in a foreign medium, and therefore involving apparent inconsistencies or mysteries." "Systematic" dogma could be "kept in the background in the infancy of Christianity, when faith and obedience were vigorous," and only "brought forward at a time when, reason being disproportionately developed, and aiming at sovereignty in the province of religion, its presence became necessary to expel an usurping idol from the house of God." From the point of view of the individual believer, to make explicit what was implicit was not necessarily desirable: "So reluctant is a well-constituted mind to reflect on its own motive principles, that the correct intellectual image, from its hardness of outline, may startle and offend those who have all along been acting upon it." But having indicated how undesirable dogmatic formulations are, Newman immediately proceeds to show how necessary they are: for the fact that "we cannot restrain the rovings of the intellect, or silence its clamorous demand for a formal statement concerning the Object of our worship," means paradoxically that the insistence that "intellectual representation should ever be subordinate to the cultivation of the religious affections" actually demands the "intellectual expression of theological truth," not only because it "excludes heresy," but because it "directly assists the acts of religious worship and obedience."[18]

In *Tract 73* (1835), later republished under the title "On the Introduction of Rationalistic Principles into Revealed Religion," Newman explains why human language is inherently incapable of expressing adequately the truths of divine revelation. "Considered as a Mystery," a revealed truth "is a doctrine enunciated by inspiration, in human language, as the only possible medium of it, and suitably, according to the capacity of language; a doctrine *lying hid* in language, to be received in that language from the first by every mind, whatever be its separate power of understanding it." He takes the necessity of verbal formulations

for granted, but he also recognizes the inevitable inadequacy
of language and the limitations of human thought. He formulates
a brilliant exposition of how mystery is involved in the idea
of revelation:

> No revelation can be complete and systematic, from the weakness
> of the human intellect; *so far as* it is not such, it is mysterious. . . .
> A Revelation is religious doctrine viewed on its illuminated side;
> a Mystery is the selfsame doctrine viewed on the side unilluminated.
> Thus Religious Truth is neither light nor darkness, but both
> together; it is like the dim view of a country seen in the twilight,
> with forms half extracted from the darkness, with broken lines,
> and isolated masses. Revelation . . . is not a revealed *system*, but
> consists of a number of detached and incomplete truths belonging
> to a vast system unrevealed, of doctrines and injunctions
> mysteriously connected together.[19]

In *Lectures on the Doctrine of Justification* (1838), doctrinal
statements are still seen as negative rather than positive.
Necessary and useful as "landmarks" and summaries of belief,
they are "intended to forbid speculations, which are sure to
spring up in the human mind, and to anticipate its attempts
at systematic views by showing the ultimate abyss at which all
rightly conducted inquiries arrive, not to tell us anything definite
and real, which we did not know before, or which is beyond
the faith of the most unlearned."[20]

By the time, however, Newman came to write the last of
the *Oxford University Sermons* on "The Theory of Developments
in Religious Doctrine" (1843), the formulation of dogmatic propositions is viewed in a more positive light, if only because doctrinal development is seen as a sign of life in the Church. It
is true that doctrinal statements are said to be "necessary only
because the human mind cannot reflect . . . except piecemeal"
upon "the one idea which they are designed to express," so that
they are only expressions of "aspects" of the "idea" and "can never
really be confused with the idea itself, which all such propositions taken together can but reach, and cannot exceed," and
indeed to which they "are never equivalent"—for "dogmas are,

after all, but symbols of a Divine fact, which, far from being compassed by those very propositions, would not be exhausted, nor fathomed, by a thousand." On the other hand, dogmatic definitions are regarded as essential for realizing the Christian revelation. There is no contradiction between a personal faith in Christ and a dogmatic creed because the latter only seeks to give expression and substance to the former:

> That idea is not enlarged, if propositions are added, nor impaired if they are withdrawn: if they are added, this is with a view of conveying that one integral view, not of amplifying it. That view does not depend on such propositions: it does not consist in them; they are but specimens and indications of it. And they may be multiplied without limit. They are necessary, but not needful to it, being but portions or aspects of that previous impression which has at length come under the cognizance of Reason and the terminology of science. . . . One thing alone has to be impressed on us by Scripture, the Catholic idea, and in it they are all included. To object, then, to the number of propositions, upon which an anathema is placed, is altogether to mistake their use; for their multiplication is not intended to enforce many things, but to express one.[21]

If this view of revelation (the "idea") seems too impersonal, then it is important to look at the later passage in the *Grammar of Assent* where Newman provides a classic statement of the relation between a personal faith and doctrinal belief. Of "the common mistake of supposing that there is a contrariety and antagonism between a dogmatic creed and vital religion," Newman is critical:

> People urge that salvation consists, not in believing the propositions that there is a God, that there is a Saviour, that our Lord is God, that there is a Trinity, but in believing in God, in a Saviour, in a Sanctifier; and they object that such propositions are but a formal and human medium destroying all true reception of the Gospel, and making religion a matter of words or of logic, instead of its having its seat in the heart. They are right so far as this, that men can and sometimes do rest in the propositions themselves

as expressing intellectual notions; they are wrong, when they maintain that men need do so or always do so. The propositions may
and must be used, and can easily be used, as the expression of facts,
not notions, and they are necessary to the mind in the same way
that language is ever necessary for denoting facts, both for ourselves
as individuals, and for our intercourse with others. Again, they
are useful in their dogmatic aspect as ascertaining and making clear
for us the truths on which the religious imagination has to rest.
Knowledge must ever precede the exercise of the affections. We
feel gratitude and love, we feel indignation and dislike, when we
have the informations actually put before us which are to kindle
those several emotions. We love our parents, as our parents, when
we know them to be our parents; we must know concerning God,
before we can feel love, fear, hope, or trust towards Him. Devotion must have its objects; those objects, as being supernatural,
when not represented to our senses by material symbols, must be
set before the mind in propositions. The formula, which embodies
a dogma for the theologian, readily suggests an object for the worshipper.[22]

We have come a long way from *The Arians*, where dogma
was seen as hardly more than a necessary evil, to a position
where doctrinal formulations are viewed as indispensable for
personal faith. It is not just that dogma protects religion from
error, but doctrinal propositions are now viewed as integral to
faith itself, which can hardly exist without some knowledge of
what it seeks to worship. Of course, Newman knew when he
wrote *The Arians* that the believer cannot worship Christ
without knowing something of his divinity; but he seemed to
have thought that it was a pity Christianity could not rest in
the simplest kind of proclamation of faith, without any dogmatic
developments at all. Thirty-seven years later, he is anxious both
to explain and to refute this attitude. Newman's final position
is that far from there necessarily being an opposition between
a personal and a propositional religion, the two should be
mutually interdependent.

But because dogmatic propositions are implied by an objective religion does not mean that it is possible, or even desirable, to list all the doctrines which a Catholic at any given time has to believe. The Church, Newman pointed out, "would be misrepresenting the real character of the dispensation" and "abdicating her function" by transferring the faith of Catholics "from resting on herself as the organ of revelation . . . simply to a code of certain definite articles or a written creed."[23] The Catholic position is that "the object of faith is *not* simply certain articles . . . contained in the dumb documents, but the whole word of God, explicit and implicit, as dispensed by His living Church."[24] A Catholic cannot itemize the contents of revelation, since

> there are many things which we know on the whole, but of which we cannot tell the boundaries. I know what is morally right, yet I cannot draw a sharp line in matters of detail between what is right and what is wrong. And so there may be points in Revelation which do not positively and undeniably command my faith, while yet there are points which certainly do.

Newman uses a striking secular analogy to describe the Church as the expounder and interpreter of revelation: it is like "a standing Apostolic committee—to answer questions, which the Apostles are not here to answer, concerning what they received and preached." But because "the Church does not know more than the Apostles knew, there are many questions which the Church cannot answer."[25] The Church, however, has to be infallible since Christianity "is no mere philosophy thrown upon the world at large, no mere quality of mind and thought, no mere beautiful and deep sentiment or subjective opinion, but a substantive message from above, guarded and preserved in a visible polity." It was because God "willed the Gospel to be a revelation acknowledged and authenticated, to be public, fixed, and permanent," that "He framed a Society of men to be its home, its instrument, and its guarantee," so that the "rulers of that Association are the legal trustees, so to say, of the sacred truths which He spoke to the Apostles by word of mouth."[26]

The Church and Scripture

Newman's study of primitive Christianity had shown him that the early Church did not use the Scriptures to teach the revelation of Christ, but rather that the Church itself taught what was to be believed, and only appealed to "Scripture in vindication of its own teaching": heretics, on the other hand, like the Arians, relied on a "private study of Holy Scripture" to elicit "a systematic doctrine from the scattered notices of the truth which Scripture contains."[27] The more Newman as an Anglican studied the Fathers, the more he became aware that the Bible was used by them to support the doctrines which they received from the Church's tradition, which was itself regarded as the interpreter of the Scriptures.

The idea that "every one may gain the true doctrines of the gospel for himself from the Bible," he called the "ultra-Protestant principle"; whereas according to the Fathers, "the unanimous witness of the whole Church" to the teaching of the apostles was "as much the voice of God" as was Scripture.[28] To insist, Newman argues, on "the Bible as the only standard of appeal in doctrinal inquiries" inevitably leads to the conclusion that "truth is but matter of opinion," since "the Bible is not so written as to force its meaning upon the reader," nor does it "carry with it its own interpretation." To be sure, Newman thought as an Anglican that the "creed can be proved entirely . . . from the Bible"—but "we take this ground only in controversy, not in teaching." And he readily admits that Christians "derive their faith" not from Scripture but from tradition.[29] Anyway there are serious problems in trying to draw doctrines directly and solely from the Bible, which, although inspired, is like other books in its "history" and in the "mode of its composition," and which in fact is "not one book" but "a great number of writings, of various persons, living at different times, put together into one, and assuming its existing form as if casually and by accident." To attempt to deduce "the true system of religion" from such an unsystematic "collection" would be like trying "to make out the history of Rome from the extant letters of some of its great politicians, and from the fragments of ancient annals, histories, law, inscriptions, and medals." The writers of the New Testament "did not sit down with a design to commit to paper all they had to say" about the gospel; they wrote with more limited, specific purposes in mind. Indeed, they themselves acknowledge that they "did not in Scripture say out all they had to say," but they actually refer to a "system" of doctrine and worship which would have survived even if Scripture had been lost. Not surprisingly, then, the "doctrines of faith" are in Scripture "only in an implicit shape."[30]

As a Catholic, Newman was to maintain that the difference between (high) Anglicans and Catholics over Scripture and tradition "is merely one of words": "We mean that not every article of faith is so contained there, that it may thence be logically proved, *independently* of the teaching and authority of the Tradition; but Anglicans mean that every article of faith is so contained there, that it may thence be proved, *provided* there be added the illustrations and compensations supplied by the Tradition."[31] This approach anticipates the teaching of the Second Vatican Council's constitution on revelation, which insists on the intimate connection of Scripture and tradition and fails to endorse the post-Tridentine "two sources" theory.

The Development of Doctrine

No account of Newman's theology of revelation would be complete without a consideration of his theory of the development of doctrine, which is undoubtedly his most important and original contribution to Catholic theology. His first sustained treatment of the subject is in his brilliant sermon "The Theory of Developments in Religious Doctrine" (1843), where he argues that the "large fabric of divinity"—which in the course of time has been "reared, irregular in its structure, and diverse in its style"—is "still, on the whole, the development of an idea, and like itself, and unlike any thing else." The study of the formulation of particular dogmas shows "how the great idea takes hold

of a thousand minds by its living force . . . so that the doctrine may rather be said to use the minds of Christians, than
to be used by them." Newman's unique ability to dramatize the
intellectual life makes the history of doctrinal development exciting in itself:

> Wonderful it is to see with what effort, hesitation, suspense, in-
> terruption,—with how many swayings to the right and to the left—
> with how many reverses, yet with what certainty of advance, with
> what precision in its march, and with what ultimate completeness,
> it has been evolved. . . . Wonderful, to see how heresy has but
> thrown that idea into fresh forms, and drawn out from it further
> developments, with an exuberance which exceeded all question-
> ing, and a harmony which baffled all criticism . . . .
>
> And this world of thought is the expansion of a few words, ut-
> tered, as if casually, by the fishermen of Galilee. . . . Reason has
> not only submitted, it has ministered to Faith; it has illustrated
> its documents; it has raised illiterate peasants into philosophers
> and divines; it has elicited a meaning from their words which their
> immediate hearers little suspected. . . . Its half sentences, its
> overflowings of language, admit of development; they have a life
> in them which shows itself in progress; a truth, which has the token
> of consistency; a reality, which is fruitful in resources; a depth,
> which extends into mystery: for they are representations of what
> is actual, and has a definite location and necessary bearings and
> a meaning in the great system of things, and a harmony in what
> it is, and a compatibility in what it involves.

In attempting to describe how development takes place,
Newman is careful to avoid assuming that revelation is given
necessarily in the form of doctrinal propositions: the apostles
received the fullness of God's revelation in the person of Christ
rather than through the revealing of propositional truths.

> Theological dogmas are propositions expressive of the judgments
> which the mind forms, or the impressions which it receives, of
> Revealed Truth. Revelation sets before it certain supernatural facts
> and actions, beings and principles; these make a certain impres-

sion or image upon it; and this impression spontaneously, or even necessarily, becomes the subject of reflection on the part of the mind itself.

Crucial to Newman's theory is the epistemological distinction he had already made in one of the earlier *Oxford University Sermons* on the difference between "Implicit and Explicit Reason." Thus, in the process of development, he insists that, "naturally as the inward idea of divine truth . . . passes into explicit form by the activity of our reflective powers, still such an actual delineation is not essential to its genuineness and perfection," so that a "peasant may have such a true impression, yet be unable to give any intelligible account of it." Indeed, the "impression made upon the mind need not even be recognized" by the person "possessing it." Such "unperceived impressions" are common in life; people may not even be "conscious" of "an idea" of which they are actually "possessed." Nor is the "absence, or partial absence, or incompleteness of dogmatic statements" any "proof of the absence of impressions or implicit judgments, in the mind of the Church. Even centuries might pass without the formal expression of a truth, which had been all along the secret life of millions of faithful souls."[32]

In the *Essay on the Development of Christian Doctrine* (1845), Newman points out that the development of doctrine has been "implicitly adopted by theologians" through the ages as a "hypothesis to account for a difficulty"—namely, that Christianity has apparently undergone so many changes and variations over the centuries that the question arises whether there has been any "real continuity of doctrine" since the time of the apostles.[33] However, although there may have been nothing particularly original about the idea of development, Newman was not only the first theologian to pay sustained attention to the subject, but his theory (if it may be called that, since it is the least "theoretical" of theories) is more complex and subtle than the two principal theories previously adopted by Catholic theologians. The Scholastics' theory of *logical explication*, which maintained that later dogmatic formulations are logically deduced from previous formulations, seems clearly too rigid for the historical facts; the French theologian Bossuet's *principle of clarification*, which regarded developments as simply explanations of doctrines already formulated—and which was more or less the view Newman himself had taken in his earlier Anglican days—hardly accounts for the great extent of development.

Newman's idea of development cannot be understood without first comprehending his concept of an "idea" and its "aspects."

The idea which represents an object or supposed object is commensurate with the sum total of its possible aspects, however they may vary in the separate consciousness of individuals; and in proportion to the variety of aspects under which it presents itself to various minds is its force and depth, and the argument for its reality. Ordinarily an idea is not brought home to the intellect as objective except through this variety; like bodily substances, which are not apprehended except under the clothing of their properties and results, and which admit of being walked round, and surveyed on opposite sides, and in different perspectives, and in contrary light, in evidence of their reality. And, as views of a material object may be taken from points so remote or so opposed, that they seem at first sight incompatible, and especially as their shadows will be disproportionate, or even monstrous, and yet all these anomalies will disappear and all these contrarieties be adjusted, on ascertaining the point of vision or the surface of projection in each case; so also all the aspects of an idea are capable of coalition, and of a resolution into the object to which it belongs; and the *prima facie* dissimilitude of its aspects becomes, when explained, an argument for its substantiveness and integrity, and their multiplicity for its originality and power.

And so there is "no one aspect deep enough to exhaust the contents of a real idea, no one aspect or proposition which will serve to define it."

Not all ideas can "properly be called living," but

when an idea, whether real or not, is of a nature to arrest and possess the mind, it may be said to have life, that is, to live in the mind which is its recipient. . . . then it is not merely received passively in this or that form into many minds, but it becomes an active principle within them, leading them to an ever-new contemplation of itself, to an application of it in various directions, and a propagation of it on every side.

A living idea grows gradually into "a body of thought," which "will after all be little more than the proper representative of one idea, being in substance what that idea meant from the first, its complete image as seen in a combination of diversified aspects, with the suggestions and corrections of many minds, and the illustration of many experiences."

It is the "process . . . by which the aspects of an idea are brought into consistency and form" that Newman calls "its development, being the germination and maturation of some truth or apparent truth on a large mental field." But "this process will not be a development, unless the assemblage of aspects, which constitute its ultimate shape, really belongs to the idea from which they start." Far from being passive,

a development will have this characteristic, that, its action being in the busy scene of human life, it cannot progress at all without cutting across, and thereby destroying or modifying and incorporating with itself existing modes of thinking and operating. The development then of an idea is not like an investigation worked out on paper, in which each successive advance is a pure evolution from a foregoing, but it is carried on through and by means of communities of men and their leaders and guides; and it employs their minds as its instruments, and depends upon them, while it uses them.

The context, too, in which the development takes place, is important: "an idea not only modifies, but is modified, or at least influenced, by the state of things in which it is carried out, and is dependent in various ways on the circumstances which surround it." There may be "the risk of corruption from intercourse with the world around," but "such a risk must be encountered if a great idea is duly to be understood, and much more if it is to be fully exhibited. It is elicited and expanded by trial, and battles into perfection and supremacy." In other words, an idea is brought out rather than obscured by development, as Newman argues in a classic passage, which concludes with one of the most frequently quoted sentences from his writings:

It is indeed sometimes said that the stream is clearest near the spring. Whatever use may fairly be made of this image, it does not apply to the history of a philosophy or belief, which on the contrary is more equable, and purer, and stronger, when its bed has become deep, and broad, and full. It necessarily rises out of an existing state of things, and for a time savours of the soil. Its vital element needs disengaging from what is foreign and temporary . . . . It remains perhaps for a time quiescent; it tries, as it were, its limbs, and proves the ground under it, and feels its way. From time to time it makes essays which fail, and are in consequence abandoned. It seems in suspense which way to go; it wavers, and at length strikes out in one definite direction. In time it enters upon strange territory; points of controversy alter their bearing; parties rise and fall around it; dangers and hopes appear in new relations; and old principles reappear under new forms. It changes with them in order to remain the same. In a higher world it is otherwise, but here below to live is to change, and to be perfect is to have changed often.[34]

Far from being unexpected, there is an "antecedent probability" in favor of developments in doctrine. After all, "If Christianity is a fact, and impresses an idea of itself on our minds and is a subject-matter of exercises of the reason, that idea will in course of time expand into a multitude of ideas, and aspects of ideas, connected and harmonious with one another, and in themselves determinate and immutable, as is the objective fact itself which is thus represented." The more an idea claims to be "living, the more various will be its aspects," for "whole objects do not create in the intellect whole ideas, but are . . . thrown . . . into a number of statements, strengthening, interpreting, correcting each other, and with more or less exact-

ness approximating, as they accumulate, to a perfect image."
It is not possible to "teach except by aspects or views, which
are not identical with the thing itself which we are teaching."

Since Christianity in particular is not a local but a universal religion, "it cannot but vary in its relations and dealings
towards the world around it, that is, it will develop," for "principles require a very various application according as persons
and circumstances vary, and must be thrown into new shapes
according to the form of society which they are to influence."
New problems and questions arise which "must be answered,
and, unless we suppose a new revelation, answered by means
of the revelation which we have, that is, by development."

Scripture, for instance, does not solve the difficulties which
are raised about its own authority and interpretation, but "in
matter of fact the decision has been left to time, to the slow
process of thought, to the influence of mind upon mind, the
issues of controversy, and the growth of opinion." And the fact
that "Scripture needs completion" suggests that the "defect or
inchoateness in its doctrines" constitutes "an antecedent probability in favour of a development of them." In the Bible itself
we find a "prophetic Revelation" in the form of "a process of
development," in which

> the earlier prophecies are pregnant texts out of which the suc-
> ceeding announcements grow; they are types. It is not that first
> one truth is told, then another; but the whole truth or large por-
> tions of it are told at once, yet only in rudiments, or in miniature,
> and they are expanded and finished in their parts, as the course
> of revelation proceeds.

The truth is that "the whole Bible, not its prophetical portions
only, is written on the principle of development. As the Revelation proceeds, it is ever new, yet ever old." Moreover, the say-
ings of Christ and the apostles

> are of a typical structure . . . predictions as well as injunctions
> of doctrine. If then the prophetic sentences have had that develop-
> ment which has really been given them, first by succeeding revela-

tions, and then by the event, it is probable antecedently that those doctrinal, political, ritual, and ethical sentences, which have the same structure, should admit the same expansion.

It is not surprising that after the ascension it is impossible "to fix an historical point at which the growth of doctrine ceased, and the rule of faith was once for all settled," or to find "one doctrine . . . which starts complete at first, and gains nothing afterwards from the investigations of faith and the attacks of heresy."[35]

If there is an antecedent probability for developments, then "this is a strong antecedent argument in favour of a provision in the Dispensation for putting a seal of authority upon those developments." After all, Christianity "is a revelation which comes to us as a revelation, as a whole, objectively, and with a profession of infallibility," for, "unlike other revelations . . . except the Jewish, of which it is a continuation, [it] is an objective religion, or a revelation with credentials."

> We are told that God has spoken. Where? In a Book? We have tried it and it disappoints; it disappoints us, that most holy and blessed gift, not from fault of its own, but because it is used for a purpose for which it was not given. . . . The Church undertakes that office; she does what none else can do, and this is the secret of her power.

Again, "a revelation is not given, if there be no authority to decide what it is that is given." And so, in order to distinguish true from false developments, a "supreme authority" is necessary—without an "infallible chair" the only unity possible is "a comprehension of opinions." Nor is "the notion of development under infallible authority" an implausible "hypothesis . . . to account for the rise of Christianity and the formation of its theology."[36]

Newman argues that "of all existing systems, the present communion of Rome is the nearest approximation in fact to the Church of the Fathers, possible though some may think it, to be nearer still to that Church on paper."

Did St. Athanasius or St. Ambrose come suddenly to life, it cannot be doubted what communion he would take to be his own.
All surely will agree that these Fathers, with whatever opinions
of their own, whatever protests, if we will, would find themselves
more at home with such men as St. Bernard or St. Ignatius Loyola,
or with the lonely priest in his lodging, or the holy sisterhood of
mercy, or the unlettered crowd before the altar, than with the
teachers or with the members of any other creed. And may we
not add, that were those same Saints, who once sojourned, one
in exile, one on embassy, at Treves, to come more northward still,
and to travel until they reached another fair city, seated among
groves, green meadows, and calm streams, the holy brothers would
turn from many a high aisle and solemn cloister which they found
there, and ask the way to some small chapel where mass was said
in the populous alley or forlorn suburb? And, on the other hand,
can any one who has but heard his name, and cursorily read his
history, doubt for one instant how, in turn, the people of England
. . . would deal with Athanasius—Athanasius, who spent his long
years in fighting against sovereigns for a theological term?[37]

The general point that there has existed since apostolic times
a continuous, developing body of doctrine called Catholicism
becomes vividly real for Newman through the concretely personal argument that it is

the nearest . . . to say the least, to the religious sentiment, and
what is called *ethos*, of the early Church, nay, to that of the Apostles
and Prophets . . . [who were] saintly and heroic men . . . more
like a Dominican preacher, or a Jesuit missionary, or a Carmelite
friar, more like St. Toribio, or St. Vincent Ferrer, or St. Francis
Xavier, or St. Alphonso Liguori, than to any individuals, or to
any classes of men, that can be found in other communions.[38]

Although Newman thinks it undeniable that modern Catholicism is "the historical continuation" of early Christianity,
it may still be objected that the "expansion" which has taken
place consists not of developments but of corruptions. It is
therefore "necessary . . . to assign certain characteristics of

faithful developments . . . as a test to discriminate between them and corruptions." But it is important first to understand what the word *corruption* means "when used literally of material substances." It cannot, for example, be used of "a stone," which "may be crushed to powder, but . . . cannot be corrupted." On the other hand, it can be applied to the human body, when it signifies "the breaking up of life, preparatory to its termina-tion." On the basis of this "analogy," Newman proposes seven "tests" or "notes"[39]

> of varying cogency, independence and applicability, to discriminate healthy developments of an idea from its state of corruption and decay, as follows:—There is no corruption if it retains one and the same type, the same principles, the same organization; if its begin-nings anticipate its subsequent phases, and its later phenomena protect and subserve its earlier; if it has a power of assimilation and revival, and a vigorous action from first to last.[40]

These notes are clearly intended to be suggestive and tentative rather than definitive and exhaustive. As such, they belong to what is really an exploratory essay rather than a systematic treatise. Newman's *Essay* offers not a theory but a *view* (to use his own favorite word) of the course of doctrinal development in the early Church, and it invites the reader to recognize cer-tain patterns that it traces in historical phenomena. The resulting picture or sketch is intended to show not only that Roman Catholicism is the heir to primitive Christianity, but that the modern Roman Catholic Church is the "image"— "almost like a photograph"—of the early Church.[41]

3

REDEMPTION

The Incarnation

Near the beginning of the *Essay on the Development of Christian Doctrine*, Newman says that if one was looking for the " 'leading idea' . . . of Christianity," round which other ideas could be grouped simply "for convenience," then he would personally "call the Incarnation the central aspect of Christianity, out of which the three main aspects of its teaching take their rise, the sacramental, the hierarchical, and the ascetic." However, he immediately modifies this by adding, "But one aspect of Revelation must not be allowed to exclude or to obscure another." Later in the book, he writes, cautiously again: "For the convenience of arrangement, I will consider the Incarnation the central truth of the gospel, and the source whence we are to draw out its principles."[1]

This was not the approach of what Newman calls "the popular theology of the day" in Protestant England, which emphasized the atonement as "the chief doctrine of the Gospel."[2] An emphasis on the crucifixion was very characteristic, of course, both of medieval Catholicism and of Tridentine Catholicism with its stress on the Mass as the sacrifice of Calvary. Newman's own tendency to give priority to the incarnation sets him apart from what was then at least the predominant tradition of western Christianity, both Catholic and Protestant, and is to be traced to the profound influence exerted on him by the Greek Fathers.

In his Christology Newman so emphasized the divinity of Christ as to risk downgrading his humanity, partly because of the influence of the Alexandrian Fathers, especially St. Athanasius, and partly because he was extremely anxious to rebut any diminution of Christ's divinity by the liberalizing theologians of the day.[3] He was accordingly careful when defining the doctrine of the incarnation:

> If we wish to express the sacred Mystery of the Incarnation accurately, we should rather say that God is man, than that man is God. Not that the latter proposition is not altogether Catholic in its wording, but the former expresses the *history* of the Economy, (if I may so call it,) and confines our Lord's personality to His divine nature, making His manhood an adjunct; whereas to say that man is God, does the contrary of both of these,—leads us to consider Him a man primarily and personally, with some vast and unknown dignity superadded, and that acquired of course after His coming into existence as man.[4]

The reference to mystery should not be taken as a merely conventional or pious way of speaking. As we have seen in our consideration of Newman's theology of revelation, the stress on mystery is an important and integral part of his theological strategy: Newman never allows us to forget the inadequacy of human language and thought that in the last analysis makes it literally impossible for us to understand how Christ could be both God and man, since such a union is unique and completely beyond our imagination. Indeed, says Newman, "it is a more overwhelming mystery even than that which is involved in the doctrine of the Trinity," for

> When the mystery of the Trinity is set before us, we see indeed that it is quite beyond our reason; but, at the same time, it is no wonder that human language should be unable to convey, and human intellect to receive, truths relating to the incommunicable and infinite essence of Almighty God. But the mystery of the Incarnation relates, in part, to subjects more level with our reason;

it lies not only in the manner how God and man is one Christ, but in the very fact that so it is.[5]

There has been a tendency in western theology to view the incarnation as virtually subordinate to the crucifixion; in other words, Christ came into this world principally in order that he might die for us on the cross. Newman's high doctrine of the incarnation is the same as the Fathers': God took to himself human nature in order that he might raise it to his own level or "deify" it, "to make us partakers of the Divine nature." Or, God became man so that "men, through brotherhood with Him, might in the end become as gods,"[6] to use the word that the Fathers dared to use. He came, says Newman, "selecting and setting apart for Himself the elements of body and soul; then, uniting them to Himself from their first origin of existence, pervading them, hallowing them by His own Divinity, spiritualizing them, and filling them with light and purity, the while they continued to be human. . . . And as they grew from day to day in their holy union, His Eternal Essence still was one with them, exalting them."[7] From this perspective, Christ's judgment is not simply that of the judge who was crucified by sinful men: rather, as a result of "taking our flesh" and thereby "raising human nature with Him,"

> Man shall judge man at the last day. So honoured is this earth, that no stranger shall judge us, but He who is our fellow, who will sustain our interests, and has full sympathy in all our imperfections. . . . He our brother will decide about His brethren.[8]

In his Catholic sermons Newman does not hesitate to ally himself with the view of Duns Scotus (as against St. Thomas Aquinas) that even had mankind never sinned, the Son of God would still have "had it in mind to come on earth among innocent creatures . . . to fill them with . . . grace, to receive their worship, to enjoy their company, and to prepare them for . . . heaven." Newman is convinced that there would have been an incarnation, although it would have taken a different form, without the fall: "He once had meant to come on earth in heavenly glory, but we sinned; and then He could not safely visit us, except with a shrouded radiance and a bedimmed Majesty, for He was God. So He came Himself in weakness, not in power."[9]

Such is the mystery of the incarnation that there is always the danger for the finite human mind of separating the divinity and the humanity of Christ. And so Newman urges that "His Divine Sonship is that portion of the sacred doctrine on which the mind is providentially intended to rest throughout, and so to preserve for itself His identity unbroken."[10] This is important because it was by no means fortuitous that it was the second person of the Trinity who became incarnate (and here Newman anticipates modern Catholic theologians like Karl Rahner who insist on distinguishing the different functions of the three persons of the Trinity, which have too often been blurred in the western tradition):

> Our Lord's Sonship is not only the guarantee to us of His Godhead, but also the condition of His incarnation. As the Son was God, so on the other hand was the Son suitably made man; it belonged to Him to have the Father's perfections, it became Him to assume a servant's form. We must beware of supposing that the Persons of the Ever-Blessed and All-holy Trinity differ from each other only in this, that the Father is not the Son, and the Son is not the Father. They differ in this besides, that the Father is the Father, and the Son is the Son. While They are one in substance, Each has distinct characteristics which the Other has not. Surely those sacred Names have a meaning in them, and must not lightly be passed over.[11]

The Crucifixion

When we turn from the incarnation to the crucifixion, we find the same stress on mystery: "Why was this suffering necessary to procure for us the blessings which we were in ourselves unworthy of? We do not know."[12] And Newman discourages inquiry: "We must not search curiously what is His present office, what is meant by His pleading His sacrifice, and by His perpetual intercession for us."[13]

But apart from Newman's extreme sensitivity to mystery, there was another reason why he especially disliked too much explicit attention to be paid to the cross of Christ, as is indicated in this warning in one of his Anglican sermons: "the sacred doctrine of the Atoning Sacrifice is not one to be talked of, but to be lived upon; not to be put forth irreverently, but to be adored secretly; not to be used as a necessary instrument in the conversion of the ungodly, or for the satisfaction of reasoners of this world."[14] Newman was reacting against an Evangelicalism, so prevalent in his own day, which likes to brandish or flourish Christ's passion in order to stimulate that faith which alone, it believes, can justify the sinner. In *The Arians* Newman maintained that Scripture offered "no . . . sanction . . . whether of precept or of example, in behalf of the practice of stimulating the affections, such as gratitude or remorse, by means of the doctrine of the Atonement, in order to the conversion of the hearers."[15] In a private letter he complained that Evangelical sermons were "hurtful" in "their rudeness, irreverence, and almost profaneness . . . of making a most sacred doctrine" like the atonement "a subject of vehement declamation, or instrument of exciting the feelings"; it was "inexpressibly" distressing to hear "our Lord's name and work used as a sort of charm or spell to convert men by."[16]

Tractarian *reserve* and sense of mystery discouraged Newman as an Anglican from speculating about "the great and awful doctrine of the Cross of Christ."[17] However, he was not totally reticent: "Human nature, fallen and corrupt, was under the wrath of God, and it was impossible that it should be restored to His favour till it had expiated its sin by suffering. Why this was necessary, we know not; but . . . The Son of God . . . took our nature on Him, that in Him it might do and suffer what in itself was impossible to it."[18] And even if it was impossible to explain the mystery, at least it was possible to "show the use of the doctrine to us sinners": "the contemplation of our guilt is so growing and so overwhelming a misery . . . that some strong act (so to call it) was necessary, on God's part, to counterbalance the tokens of His wrath which are around us, to calm and reassure us, and to be the ground and the medium of our faith."[19]

It has often been pointed out that Newman's conversion to Catholicism had in various ways a liberating effect on him, and it does seem that in his Catholic preaching he felt freer actually to speculate about God's motives for the atonement. Thus in one sermon he is prepared to suggest that the reason why Christ suffered and died for our sins, although God could have saved the world in any way he liked, is that God the Father "has done, not what was possible merely, but what was best. And this is why the coming of the Word was necessary; for if a true satisfaction was to be made, then nothing could accomplish this, short of the incarnation of the All-holy." Christ's passion is the supreme example of "voluntary suffering":

> He came to die when He need not have died; He died to satisfy for what might have been pardoned without satisfaction; He paid a price which need not have been asked. . . . He died, not in order to exert a peremptory claim on the Divine justice, if I may so speak,—as if He were bargaining in the market-place, or pursuing a plea in a court of law,—but in a more loving, generous, munificent way, did He shed that blood.

One drop would have been enough for all the sins of the world, but "it is as if He delighted in having to suffer; as if He wished to show all creatures, what would otherwise have seemed impossible, that the Creator could practise, in the midst of His heavenly blessedness, the virtues of a creature, self-abasement and humility." There is nothing more mystifying to finite human beings than the infinitude of God, and yet Newman finds a reason for the crucifixion in that very mystery: "What would be profusion and extravagance in man, is but suitable or necessary, if I may say so, in Him whose resources are illimitable. . . . He cannot do a small work; He cannot act by halves; He ever does whole works, great works."[20] To speak so personally about God would surely have seemed to the Anglican Newman overly familiar, if not irreverent: awe at the mystery would have demanded greater distance. As an Anglican, he had criticized those, for example, who "suggested that the vicarious satisfaction of Christ acts as a salutary lesson, how severe God might be to those who sin, did they receive their deserts, a lesson to all races of intellectual beings, present and to come, in order to the stability of His moral government."[21]

One of the best of the Catholic sermons is the remarkable "Mental Sufferings of Our Lord in His Passion," in which Newman, with great reverence and sensitivity, explores the nature of Christ's suffering on the cross. He begins by pointing out that animals cannot feel pain in the same way that human beings do "because they cannot reflect on what they feel; they have no advertence or direct consciousness of their sufferings. This it is that makes pain so trying, viz., that we cannot help thinking of it, while we suffer it." This is why, Newman argues with considerable psychological acumen, human beings in intense agony feel

> that they have borne *as much* as they can bear; as if the continuance and not the intenseness was what made it too much for them. What does this mean, but that the memory of the foregoing moments of pain acts upon and (as it were) edges the pain that succeeds? If the third or fourth or twentieth moment of pain could be taken by itself, if the succession of the moments that preceded it could be forgotten, it would be no more than the first moment, as bearable as the first (taking away the shock which accompanies the first); but what makes it unbearable is, that it *is* the twentieth. . . . It is the intellectual comprehension of pain, as a whole diffused through successive moments, which gives it its special power and keenness, and it is the soul only, which a brute has not, which is capable of that comprehension.

Newman now applies his analogy to the suffering of Christ:

> Do you recollect their offering Him wine mingled with myrrh, when He was on the point of being crucified? He would not drink

of it; why? because such a potion would have stupified His mind, and He was bent on bearing the pain in all its bitterness. . . . He did not turn away His face from the suffering; He confronted it, or, as I may say, He breasted it, that every particular portion of it might make its due impression on Him. And as men are superior to brute animals, and are affected by pain more than they, by reason of the mind within them, which gives a substance to pain, such as it cannot have in the instance of brutes; so, in like manner, our Lord felt pain of the body, with an advertence and a consciousness, and therefore with a keenness and intensity, and with a unity of perception, which none of us can possibly fathom or compass, because His soul was so absolutely in His power, so simply free from the influence of distractions, so fully directed *upon* the pain, so utterly surrendered, so simply subjected to the suffering. And thus He may truly be said to have suffered the whole of His passion in every moment of it.[22]

Newman may seem practically to deny the humanity of Christ when he says that Christ was in complete control of his passion:

The soul of other men is subjected to its own wishes, feelings, impulses, passions, perturbations; His soul was subjected simply to His Eternal and Divine Personality. Nothing happened to His soul by chance, or on a sudden; He never was taken by surprise; nothing affected Him without His willing beforehand that it should affect Him.

But what is so striking is that the conclusion Newman draws from the fully voluntary nature of Christ's suffering is that Christ suffered *in his humanity* far more than he could have done if he had been *only* a human being. In other words, instead of his divinity diminishing his pain on the cross, it actually caused a thoroughly human pain utterly in excess of anything we can conceive of. To the obvious objection that Christ could not have suffered as much as an ordinary human being would if he was the Son of God and knew he was, Newman's reply is that the opposite was true, namely that Christ suffered so much in his humanity precisely because of his divinity.

As the whole of His body, stretched out upon the Cross, so the whole of His soul, His whole advertence, His whole consciousness, a mind awake, a sense acute, a living co-operation, a present, absolute intention, not a virtual permission, not a heartless submission, this did He present to His tormentors. His passion was an action; He lived most energetically, while He lay languishing, fainting, and dying. Nor did He die, except by an act of the will; for He bowed His head, in command as well as in resignation, and said, "Father, into Thy hands I commend My Spirit;" He gave the word, He surrendered His soul, He did not lose it.

The last two sentences might seem to impugn the reality of Christ's humanity, but Newman is clear and emphatic that this is not the case:

God was the sufferer; God suffered in His human nature; the sufferings belonged to God, and were drunk up, were drained out to the bottom of the chalice, because God drank them; not tasted or sipped, not flavoured, disguised by human medicaments, as man disposes of the cup of anguish.

Just as human suffering is greater than animal suffering because of human consciousness, so Christ's passion was of an extraordinary nature because of its unique psychological character— "He walks forth into a mental agony with as definite an action as if it were some bodily torture." Christ's suffering, Newman claims, was essentially mental rather than bodily suffering. In answer to the argument that one would expect Christ to "be supported under His trial by the consciousness of innocence and the anticipation of triumph," Newman counters that in fact "his trial consisted in the withdrawal, as of other causes of consolation, so of that very consciousness and anticipation." And "as men of self-command can turn from one thought to another at their will, so much more did He deliberately deny Himself the comfort, and satiate Himself with the woe."

Having argued that Christ's psychological suffering was uniquely painful, Newman now comes to the paradoxical conclusion that the actual experience that caused such terrible

anguish was the kind of experience that ordinary human beings experience with comparative indifference:

> He had to bear what is well known to us, what is familiar to us,
> but what to Him was woe unutterable. He had to bear that which
> is so easy a thing to us, so natural, so welcome, that we cannot
> conceive of it as of a great endurance, but which to Him had the
> scent and the poison of death—He had . . . to bear the weight
> of sin . . . He had to bear the sin of the whole world.

And Newman concludes the sermon by attributing Christ's
death not to physical causes but to mental suffering: "And then,
when the appointed moment arrived, and He gave the word,
as His Passion had begun with His soul, with the soul did it
end. He did not die of bodily exhaustion, or of bodily pain;
at His will His tormented Heart broke, and He commended
His Spirit to the Father."[23]

The Resurrection and Pentecost

Too often in the past, western theology has regarded the
resurrection as a kind of happy ending to the real drama that
took place on the cross, and its importance has been neglected
in Christ's work of redemption. Catholic theology in this century has come to appreciate that the idea that the resurrection
merely attests to Christ's divinity and his victory over sin is
a very impoverished version of the theology of the New Testament and the Fathers. But long before F. X. Durrwell's epoch-
making study *The Resurrection* (1950), Newman's own scriptural
and patristic studies had shown him that "those who omit the
Resurrection in their view of the divine economy, are as really
defective in faith as if they omitted the Crucifixion. On the
Cross He paid the debt of the world, but as He could not have
been crucified without first taking flesh, so again He could not
. . . apply His Atonement without first rising again."[24]
Newman criticized Evangelicals who "think individuals are
justified immediately by the great Atonement,—justified by

Christ's death, and not, as St. Paul says, by means of His Resurrection."[25] The real reason, he says, that the apostles preached the resurrection "as if it were the main doctrine of the Gospel" is that the resurrection is "the means by which the Atonement is applied to each of us."[26]

Not that Newman ignored the more obvious, external aspects of the resurrection: he preached, for example, that "the very reason *why* Christ showed Himself at all was in order to raise up *witnesses* to His resurrection, ministers of His word, founders of His Church"; for "the real object of His rising again" was "the propagation of His Gospel through the world."[27] But there were deeper reasons, more fundamental to our redemption. Through the incarnation, human nature was "renewed" in Christ, "glorious and wonderful beyond our thoughts"; as a result of the resurrection this same nature was raised up in glory, so that "Henceforth, we dare aspire to enter into the heaven of heavens, and to live for ever in God's presence, because the first-fruits of our race is already there in the Person of His Only-begotten Son."[28]

A sermon for Christmas contains a lyrical, even sublime passage where Newman celebrates the great mysteries of the redemption:

He died, to rise again the third day, the Sun of Righteousness, fully displaying that splendour which had hitherto been concealed by the morning clouds. He rose again, to ascend to the right hand of God, there to plead His sacred wounds in token of our forgiveness, to rule and guide His ransomed people, and from His pierced side to pour forth His choicest blessings upon them. He ascended, thence to descend again in due season to judge the world which He has redeemed. – Great is our Lord, and great is His power, Jesus the Son of God and Son of man. Ten thousand times more dazzling bright than the highest Archangel, is our Lord and Christ. By birth the Only-begotten and Express image of God; and in taking our flesh, not sullied thereby, but raising human nature with Him, as He rose from the lowly manger to the right hand of power, – raising human nature, for Man has redeemed us, Man is set above all creatures, as one with the Creator, Man shall judge man at the last day.[29]

Three points are worth noticing about this passage. First, the preacher clearly does not envisage Christ's work of redemption as completed on the cross. Second, far from the resurrection being an essentially spiritual event, simply confirming the victory of the cross, the raising of Christ's body in glory is seen, like his original fleshly incarnation, as a crucial part of our redemption. Third, Newman, like modern theologians, emphasizes that the crucifixion, resurrection, ascension, and pentecost are to be seen not so much as separate events and actions but as constituting one single divine act unfolding in several closely connected stages.

In a sermon for Easter day Newman shows the close connection between the incarnation and the resurrection—"Corruption had no power over that Sacred Body, the fruit of a miraculous conception." When Christ was raised from the dead, "the Divine Essence streamed forth (so to say) on every side, and environed His Manhood, as in a cloud of glory. So transfigured was His Sacred Body, that He who had deigned to be born of a woman, and to hang upon the cross, had subtle virtue in Him, like a spirit, to pass through the closed doors to His assembled followers."[30] But if the resurrection completes the incarnation, it also leads directly to the ascension, for when Christ was raised from the dead he was at the same time raised up in glory to the Father. And it was necessary that the post-resurrection appearances should cease and that Christ should leave this world in order that we might receive the Holy Spirit: "We are able to see that the Saviour, when once He entered into this world, never so departed as to suffer things to be as they were before He came; for He is still with us, not in mere gifts, but by the substitution of His Spirit for Himself, and that, both in the Church, and in the souls of individual Christians."[31]

Pentecost applied the resurrection to our human situation in the sense that the risen and glorified Christ became savingly present to each individual Christian as well as to the whole

Church through the Holy Spirit. "Christ's bodily presence, which was limited to place," had to be "exchanged for the manifold spiritual indwelling of the Comforter within us."[32] The Son returned to the Father, and in his place came "the Eternal Love whereby the Father and the Son have dwelt in each other,"[33] the Holy Spirit, the third person of the Trinity. Newman insists that "the Holy Ghost's coming is so really His coming, that we might as well say that He was not here in the days of His flesh, when He was visibly in this world, as deny that He is here now, when He is here by His Divine Spirit."[34] This new presence was necessary, for "the Spirit came to finish in us, what Christ had finished in Himself, but left unfinished as regards us. To Him it is committed to apply to us severally all that Christ had done for us." Through the Spirit, Christ's redemption comes to each one of us: "What was actually done by Christ in the flesh eighteen hundred years ago, is in type and resemblance really wrought in us one by one even to the end of time."

Newman's theology of the work of the Holy Spirit in Christ's redemption is eloquently comprehensive: Christ

> was born of the Spirit, and we too are born of the Spirit. He was justified by the Spirit, and so are we. He was pronounced the well-beloved Son, when the Holy Ghost descended on Him; and we too cry Abba, Father, through the Spirit sent into our hearts. He was led into the wilderness by the Spirit; He did great works by the Spirit; He offered himself to death by the Eternal Spirit; He was raised from the dead by the Spirit; He was declared to be the Son of God by the Spirit of holiness on His resurrection: we too are led by the same Spirit into and through this world's temptations; we, too, do our works of obedience by the Spirit; we die from sin, we rise again unto righteousness through the Spirit; and we are declared to be God's sons,—declared, pronounced, dealt with as righteous,—through our resurrection unto holiness in the Spirit. . . . Christ Himself vouchsafes to repeat in each of us in figure and mystery all that He did and suffered in the flesh. He is formed in us, born in us, suffers in us, rises again in us, lives

in us; and this not by a succession of events, but all at once: for he comes to us as a Spirit, all dying, all rising again, all living.[35]

The Holy Spirit unites us not only to the Son but also to the Father, "for He who once was on earth, has now departed from this visible scene of things in a mysterious, twofold way, both to His Father and into our hearts, thus making the Creator and His creatures one." Again Newman insists that the Spirit does not replace or substitute for the Son:

> Let us not for a moment suppose that God the Holy Ghost comes in such sense that God the Son remains away. No; He has not so come that Christ does not come, but rather He comes that Christ may come in His coming. Through the Holy Ghost we have communion with Father and Son. . . . The Holy Spirit causes, faith welcomes, the indwelling of Christ in the heart. Thus the Spirit does not take the place of Christ in the soul, but secures that place to Christ.[36]

Justification

Newman had discovered for himself in the New Testament and the Fathers the great forgotten doctrine of the indwelling in the soul of the Holy Spirit, and through the Spirit of the Father and the Son as well. It had, after all, been

> the great promise of the Gospel, that the Lord of all, who had hitherto manifested Himself externally to His servants, should take up His abode in their hearts. . . . Though He had come in our flesh, so as to be seen and handled, even this was not enough. Still He was external and separate; but after His ascension He descended again by and in His Spirit, and then at length the promise was fulfilled.[37]

Our redemption was then complete: the "dreadful reality" of original sin was overtaken by a "new righteousness," a "real righteousness" which "comes from the Holy and Divine Spirit," so that our "works, done in the Spirit of Christ, have a justifying *principle* in them, and that is the presence of the All-holy Spirit," which "hallows those acts, that life, that obedience of which it is the original cause, and which it orders and fashions."[38] This "gift of the Spirit" is gained by "faith in Christ."

While, then, Newman preaches that without faith there can be no justification of the sinner, he disagrees with Evangelicals who "consider it as a state, not of holiness and righteousness, but merely or mainly of acceptance with God."[39] For him "faith gains the promise, and . . . the promise is the great gift of the Spirit."[40] But while "faith is a condition of Christ's grace," it is not "a token"; and somebody "may have true faith, and still not yet be justified," since having "faith" is not the same as enjoying the "promise." Evangelicals, on the other hand, "consider justification to be nothing more than God's *accounting* them righteous, which is just what justification was to the Jews. Justification *is* God's accounting a man righteous; yes, but it is, in the case of the Christian, something more; it is God's *making* him righteous too." Just as "the presence of a soul is the mode in which God gives man life, so the presence of the Holy Spirit is the mode in which God gives him righteousness."[41] Again, unlike Evangelicals, Catholic Christians agree with pagans and Jews that "works are the means of salvation," only differing "in respect to the quality of these works."[42]

In his Anglican *Lectures on the Doctrine of Justification* (1838), a pioneering classic of ecumenical theology, Newman tackles the notorious problem of justification which had divided, and still to some extent divides, Catholics and Protestants. He criticizes both the "erroneous" idea of justification by "faith only" and the "defective" theory of "justification by obedience" which he attributes to "extreme" Roman Catholic theologians. He admits, however, that these two "rigid" and "extreme" views are both partially right, for the idea that "we are absolutely saved by obedience, that is, by *what we are*, has introduced the proper merit of good works; that we are absolutely saved by faith, or by *what Christ is*, the notion that good works are not conditions of our salvation."[43]

Evangelical theology assumes that "justifying faith" will always be "lively" and "lead to good works"; but it is quite possible to believe fully that one has been saved by Christ "without any fruit following": "Trusting faith is not necessarily living faith." The explanation that the "life of faith" must be "love" is rejected by Evangelicals on the ground that this would "deny the innate life and power of faith as such, and . . . associate another principle with it as a joint instrument in justification."[44] Instead, they claim that justifying faith is defined "not by what *it is*, but by what it *does*," for it is "trust *in Christ*, and it differs from all other kinds of faith in That towards which it reaches forward and on which it rests." Such a faith hardly "admits of a definition," but derives "its character" and "its form" from the "Object of the faith . . . which makes the faith what it is." Newman criticizes the evasiveness of the explanation: "They seem to allow that faith *is* in itself something more than trust, though men may be unable to say what it is more."[45] They assert that faith "*sees* the purchased redemption, and therefore must be able to *take* and *apply* it": in other words, "it *apprehends* Christ; a suitable, or rather convenient term as vaguely including both ideas, of accepting the message and receiving the gift, without making the distinction between them."[46]

To the objection that "the thought of Christ may be possessed by those who have not Christ, and therefore that it is in no sense the form or characteristic principle of justifying faith; rather that love . . . is the true form, the discriminating mark and moulding principle under which belief is converted into Faith and made justifying," the Evangelical answer is that such a doctrine "makes our thoughts centre on ourselves . . . fixes our faith on that love with which it is supposed to be instinct, instead of its mounting up worthless, rude, and unformed, to receive subsistence, fashion, and acceptableness in Christ."[47] The "wish to extirpate all notions of human merit" and "to give peace and satisfaction to the troubled conscience" accounts for the vehement insistence on a doctrine which arose from "opposition to the Roman doctrine concerning good works."[48] Faith, on this view, "is the instrument by which" Christ's "Righteousness becomes ours," for "He is our Righteousness, in the sense of His obedience being the substitute for ours in the sight of God's justice," with the result that "every believer has at once a perfect righteousness, yet not his own," which "precludes all boasting" because "it is not his own" and "all anxiety" because "it is perfect": "The conscience is unladen, without becoming puffed up."[49] The "doctrine of faith as the instrument, and Christ's righteousness as the form, of justification" is supposed "to secure us against self-contemplation" and all forms of self-reliance, as well as destroying "the state of doubt about our justification which must ever attend the belief that it depends on our graces and works."[50] The fact that faith makes Christ's fulfillment of the moral law ours as well "places us above the Law." It is true that Christians will obey the moral law and be "fruitful in good works," but only "naturally" as a result of faith, and not out of a sense of duty or conscience.[51]

Newman now turns "to consider the opposite scheme of doctrine, which is not unsound or dangerous in itself, but in a certain degree incomplete,—truth, but not the whole truth," insofar as it must not be "detached and isolated" from "other truths." This is the traditional view that "justification consists in love, or sanctity, or obedience," and that to be justified is not just to be counted righteous but actually to be made righteous— "not a change merely in God's dealings towards us, like the pale and wan sunshine of a winter's day, but . . . the possession of Himself."[52] Protestants "entrench themselves in a few favourite texts," but unlike the "one or two texts only, detached from their context" of Protestantism, the whole of Scripture testifies to this "actual inherent righteousness" which is "not a shadow but a substance, not a name but a power, not an imputation but an inward work."[53]

As usual, Newman has one decisive consideration: "It is what the rival doctrine is not, a real doctrine, and contains an intelligible, tangible, practical view which one can take and use."[54] By contrast, the Protestant "idea of faith" is damned as "a mere theory," from which it follows that "their whole theology is shadowy and unreal." The theme of reality is developed with superbly telling imagery:

The one view then differs from the other as the likeness of a man differs from the original. The picture resembles him; but it is not he. It is not a reality, it is all surface. It has no depth, no substance; touch it, and you will find it is not what it pretends to be. . . . I wish to deal with things, not with words. I do not look to be put off with a name or a shadow. I would treat of faith as it is actually found in the soul; and I say it is as little an isolated grace, as a man is a picture. It has a depth, a breadth, and a thickness; it has an inward life which is something over and above itself; it has a heart, and blood, and pulses, and nerves, though not upon the surface. . . . Love and fear and obedience are not really posterior to justifying faith for even a moment of time, unless bones or muscles are formed after the countenance and complexion. It is as unmeaning to speak of living faith, as being independent of newness of mind, as of solidity as divisible from body, or tallness from stature, or colour from the landscape. As well might it be said that an arm or a foot can exist out of the body, and that man is born with only certain portions, head or heart, and that the rest accrues afterwards, as that faith comes first and gives birth to other graces.

In short, just as "the presence of the soul changes the nature of the dust of the earth, and makes it flesh and blood . . . so love is the modelling and harmonizing principle on which justifying faith depends, and in which it exists and acts."[55]

According to Newman, the word *justifying* means literally " 'counting righteous,' but includes *under* its meaning 'making righteous.' "[56] By "calling righteous what is not righteous till He calls it so," God not only declares we are justified, but "He *justifies* us."[57] After all, it would be "a strange paradox to say that a thing is not because He says it is."[58] Rather, it is characteristic of God's word in Scripture that it "effects what it announces."[59] Justification, then, means both God's "'*justifying*" and man's "'*being justified*," just as "work" means "both the doing and the thing done"; and while it is possible to use it in the first active sense only or in the second passive sense only, in reality there should be no attempt to separate "the seal and the impression, justification and renewal."[60]

In his final analysis of what "our state of justification . . . consists in," Newman dismisses both theories of justification—by faith and by works—as superficial and unsatisfactory. If "the inward principle of acceptance" is held to be faith, then "the question rises, what gives to faith its acceptableness?" And the answer must be that faith rather than unbelief is "acceptable" because the former has "a something in it" that the latter does not, namely, "God's grace." So we are driven to the conclusion that "having that grace or that presence, and not faith, which is its result, must be the real token, the real state of a justified man." Conversely, "if we say that justification consists in a supernatural quality imparted to the soul by God's grace, as Roman Catholics say, then in like manner, the question arises" whether "this renovating principle" does not necessarily involve "grace itself, as an immediate divine power or presence." But if so, "then surely the possession of that grace is really our justification, and not renewal, or the principle of renewal." It can thus be shown, "by tracing farther back the lines of thought on which these apparently discordant views are placed," how they in fact "converge" in "an inward divine presence or grace, of which both faith and spiritual renovation are fruits."

Having incisively and penetratingly cut through the tangled thicket of a controversy deeply rooted in a late medieval scholastic theology of grace that had lost touch with scriptural and patristic sources, Newman can now put forward a solution that transcends both rival positions and whose brilliant originality lies simply in the rediscovery of the central New Testament doctrine of the indwelling of the Holy Spirit: "the presence of the Holy Ghost shed abroad in our hearts, the Author both of faith and of renewal, this is really that which makes us righteous, and . . . our righteousness is the possession of that presence." Justification, then, "is wrought by the power of the Spirit, or rather by His presence within us," while "faith and renewal are both present also, but as fruits of it."[61] The "connection" between "justification and renewal" is that they are "both included in that one great gift of God, the indwelling of Christ" through the Holy Spirit "in the Christian soul," which constitutes "our justification and sanctification, as its necessary results"—"And the one cannot be separated from the other except in idea, unless the sun's rays can be separated from the sun, or the power of purifying from fire or water."[62] Faith, on the other hand, as the "correlative" to God's grace, is first the "condition" and then the "instrument" of justification, while "love is the modelling and harmonizing principle on which justifying faith depends, and in which it exists and acts."[63]

4

MARY

The Anglican Sermons

Perhaps nothing is more likely to surprise a Catholic reader of Newman's Anglican sermons than his early understanding of Mary's role in our redemption. To begin with, Newman was not persuaded by the usual Protestant objection that Scripture does not support any special emphasis on Mary. He agrees in an early (1832) sermon, "The Reverence due to the Virgin Mary," that it is surprising that we do not hear more about her than what the Gospels tell us, but he argues that "Scripture was written, not to exalt this or that particular Saint, but to give glory to Almighty God." He points out that there must have been "thousands of holy souls in the times of which the Bible history treats, whom we know nothing of, because their lives did not fall upon the lines of God's public dealings with man." For example, we know that St. John the Evangelist was especially close to Jesus, but we hear little of him compared to St. Paul who was "the more illustrious propagator and dispenser of His Truth." Certainly, Christ

> has hid from us the knowledge of His more sacred and familiar feelings, His feelings towards His Mother and His friend. These were not to be exposed, as unfit for the world to know,—as dangerous, because not admitting of being known, without a risk

59

lest the honour which those Saints received through grace should eclipse in our minds the honour of Him who honoured them. Had the blessed Mary been more fully disclosed to us in the heavenly beauty and sweetness of the spirit within her, true, *she* would have been honoured, *her* gifts would have been clearly seen; but, at the same time, the Giver would have been somewhat less contemplated, because no design or work of His would have been disclosed in her history. She would have seemingly been introduced for *her* sake, not for His sake. When a Saint is seen working *towards* an end appointed by God, we *see* him to be a mere instrument, a servant though a favoured one; and though we admire him, yet, after all, we glorify God in him. We pass on *from* him to the work to which he ministers. But, when any one is introduced, full of gifts, yet without visible and immediate subserviency to God's designs, such a one seems revealed for his own sake.

But even in this sermon predating the Tractarian movement, Newman shows himself uneasily aware that "St. Mary" is no ordinary saint, for "Christ derived His manhood from her, and so had an especial unity of nature with her." Here Newman feels it would be "perhaps impossible for us to dwell much upon" this "wondrous relationship between God and man"; nevertheless, he thinks he is bound to say that "she is raised above the condition of sinful beings, though by nature a sinner." He admits the apparent anomaly: "she is brought near to God, yet is but a creature, and seems to lack her fitting place in our limited understandings, neither too high nor too low." The rule he proposes is that, "following the example of Scripture, we had better only think of her with and for her Son, never separating her from Him." In addition, this close association helps to highlight the humanity of Jesus, "for nothing is so calculated to impress on our minds that Christ is really partaker of our nature, and in all respects man, save sin only, as to associate Him with the thought of her, by whose ministration He became our brother."[1]

Newman has already in this early sermon implicitly grasped the essence of a balanced and orthodox Mariology: that in spite of the unique mediatorial role of Christ, nevertheless God used Mary as an instrument in accomplishing our redemption. The equivocation over Mary's sinfulness is highly significant, as Newman has already clearly glimpsed the need for a doctrine like the immaculate conception. Just before the passage already quoted, he asks boldly, "Who can estimate the holiness and perfection of her, who was chosen to be the Mother of Christ?" And, he continues, not only did Mary have the immense privilege and responsibility of bringing up Jesus as her son: "This contemplation runs to a higher subject, did we dare follow it; for what, think you, was the sanctified state of that human nature, of which God formed His sinless Son . . . ?"[2]

Preaching eight years later (in 1840), Newman dares to say explicitly what he had not dared to say before—"a pure and spotless Virgin brought forth God." In fact, he had come very close to referring to Mary in the same way six years before (in 1834) in a sermon for Christmas Day, when he says that, "since our nature was corrupt since Adam's fall," Christ "did not come in the way of nature, He did not clothe Himself in that corrupt flesh which Adam's race inherits." But the point is specifically linked to Mary's virginal conception: "All Adam's children are children of wrath; so our Lord came as the Son of Man, but not the son of sinful Adam. He had no earthly father." Newman does not, however, stop there. If it was necessary that Christ should not owe his birth to the will of a human father, it was equally imperative that the human mother who conceived and bore him should not be like other mothers: "He came by a new and living way; not, indeed, formed out of the ground, as Adam was at the first, lest He should miss the participation of our nature, but selecting and purifying unto Himself a tabernacle out of that which existed." Without actually calling Mary immaculate, Newman speaks of Christ as "the immaculate 'seed of the woman,' deriving His manhood from the substance of the Virgin Mary," thereby apparently implying that the flesh from which Jesus was born was itself immaculate. At this comparatively early date Newman immediately draws back from the obvious conclusion to his argument by saying: "Mary, His mother, was a sinner as others, and born of sinners." Aware, however, of the inconsistency, he adds equivocally: "but she was set apart . . . to yield a created nature to Him who was her Creator."[4]

Just as St. Paul had drawn a parallel between Adam and Christ, so the early Fathers saw Mary as the second Eve. This patristic comparison is found in Newman as early as the 1832 sermon: "in her the curse pronounced on Eve was changed to a blessing. Eve was doomed to bear children in sorrow; but now this very dispensation, in which the token of Divine anger was conveyed, was made the means by which salvation came into the world."[5]

The Anglican preacher also virtually proclaimed the doctrine of the assumption when he spoke of perhaps learning "a lesson from the deep silence which Scripture observes concerning the Blessed Virgin after the Resurrection; as if she, who was too pure and holy a flower to be more than seen here on earth, even during the season of her Son's humiliation, was altogether drawn by the Angels within the veil on His Resurrection, and had her joy in Paradise."[6] The meaning may be veiled, but the implication is clear enough.

The Catholic Writings

In the first volume of sermons that Newman published as a Catholic, *Discourses Addressed to Mixed Congregations* (1849), two of the eighteen sermons are devoted to Mary. Newman feels no need now, of course, for any hesitation or caution in drawing out explicitly what formerly he had left ambiguous or implicit.

That Mary was an instrument in the plan of salvation does not mean she had a simply passive role. Tradition, not to say Scripture, is clear that her active cooperation was essential for the incarnation. The Fathers teach that her faith and obedience to God were more important than the fact that she was the mother of Jesus. As Newman explains,

This is what is implied in Christ's answer to the woman in the crowd, who cried out, when He was preaching, "Blessed is the womb that bore Thee, and the breasts which Thou hast sucked." He replied by pointing out to His disciples a higher blessedness; "Yea, rather, blessed," He said, "are they who hear the word of God and keep it."

Far from intending to disparage his mother's importance, as Protestants have often thought, these words signify that her "obedience was in a higher state of privilege than her being His Mother; she was more blessed in her detachment from creatures, in her devotion to God, in her virginal purity, in her fulness of grace, than in her maternity."[7]

Newman takes some pains to demythologize the immaculate conception, in the sense of showing that it is not some weird and wonderful doctrine. Mary, he points out, "is a specimen, and more than a specimen, in the purity of her soul and body, of what man was before his fall, and what he would have been, had he risen to his full perfection." Mary is unique in her preservation from original sin, but by the same token she is simply the "one instance" of "what the Creator had intended" the human race "to be in its original state." Mary was no different from Adam in that she received grace from the moment of her creation; she was unlike him in that grace was "given from the first in still ampler measure . . . and she never incurred, in fact, Adam's deprivation." If it was possible for Adam to "have kept himself from sin in his first state, much more shall we expect immaculate perfection in Mary." Newman can now afford to be much more specific, even literally so, in insisting that Christ could not have been born of sinful flesh. Indeed, Jesus must have even physically looked like Mary:

> He imbibed, He absorbed into His Divine Person, her blood and the substance of her flesh; by becoming man of her, He received her lineaments and features, as the appropriate character in which He was to manifest Himself to mankind. The child is like the parent, and we may well suppose that by His likeness to her was manifested her relationship to Him.[8]

Given Mary's sinlessness and immaculate conception, it was only fitting that "she should be taken up into heaven and not lie in the grave till Christ's second coming." More extraordinary than the assumption of Mary body and soul would have been an ordinary death and burial:

> I say, it would be a greater miracle if, her life being what it was, her death was like that of other men, than if it were such as to correspond to her life. Who can conceive . . . that God should so repay the debt, which He condescended to owe to His Mother, for the elements of His human body, as to allow the flesh and blood from which it was taken to moulder in the grave? . . . Or who can conceive that that virginal frame, which never sinned, was to undergo the death of a sinner?

The official dogma of the assumption (defined in 1950 by Pope Pius XII) is silent on the question of whether Mary actually died or not before being assumed into heaven. She did, like Jesus, die, Newman assumes in this sermon; but he delicately indicates that her death was not like the death of other human beings. On the one hand, "she died, as she suffered, because she was in this world, because she was in a state of things in which suffering and death are the rule." On the other hand, Newman likes to think that because of her immaculate conception she "died not as others die" but was

> saved from disease and malady, and all that weakens and decays the bodily frame. Original sin had not been found in her, by the wear of her senses, and the waste of her frame, and the decrepitude of years, propagating death. She died, but her death was a mere fact, not an effect; and, when it was over, it ceased to be.

Although Newman receives the doctrine as part of tradition rather than as a defined dogma, he comments that,

> viewed in the light of reason, it is the *fitness* of this termination of her earthly course which so persuasively recommends it to our minds: we feel it "ought" to be; that it "becomes" her Lord and Son thus to provide for one who was so singular and special, both

in herself and her relations to Him. We find that it is simply in harmony with the substance and main outlines of the doctrine of the Incarnation, and that without it Catholic teaching would have a character of incompleteness, and would disappoint our pious expectations.[9]

Newman's fullest thinking on the place of Mary in the Christian faith is to be found in his *Letter to Pusey* (1866). He begins there by acknowledging that devotion to her among Catholics has grown over the centuries, while claiming that no growth in doctrine has occurred. He makes the point with a vivid image:

> The sun in the spring-time will have to shine many days before he is able to melt the frost, open the soil, and bring out the leaves; yet he shines out from the first notwithstanding, though he makes his power felt but gradually. It is one and the same sun, though his influence day by day becomes greater; and so in the Catholic Church it is the one Virgin Mother, one and the same from first to last, and Catholics may have ever acknowledged her; and yet, in spite of that acknowledgement, their devotion to her may be scanty in one time and place, and overflowing in another.[10]

Theologically speaking, it was St. Athanasius who first "brought the circumstances of the Incarnation home to men's minds, by the multiform evolutions of his analysis," and thus "engraved indelibly upon the imaginations of the faithful, as had never been before, that man is God, and God is man, that in Mary they meet, and that in that sense Mary is the centre of all things." And so Athanasius in the fourth century "laid the foundations" of future devotion to Mary.[11]

The teaching of the Fathers from the earliest times held that Mary is "the Second Eve." Eve took the initiative in offering the fruit of the forbidden tree to Adam: "She co-operated, not as an irresponsible instrument, but intimately and personally in the sin: she brought it about." According to Genesis,

> In that awful transaction there were three parties concerned,— the serpent, the woman, and the man; and at the time of their sentence, an event was announced for a distant future, in which

the three same parties were to meet again, the serpent, the woman, and the man; but it was to be a second Adam and a second Eve, and the new Eve was to be the mother of the new Adam. "I will put enmity between thee and the woman, and between thy seed and her seed." The Seed of the woman is the Word Incarnate, and the Woman, whose seed or son He is, is His mother Mary. This interpretation, and the parallelism it involves . . . is the doctrine of the Fathers, from the earliest times; and, this being established, we are able, by the position and office of Eve in our fall, to determine the position and office of Mary in our restoration.[12]

Newman's Mariology, then, is deeply scriptural and patristic. And he shows how the Fathers

do not speak of the Blessed Virgin merely as the physical instrument of our Lord's taking flesh, but as an intelligent, responsible cause of it; her faith and obedience being accessories to the Incarnation, and gaining it as her reward. As Eve failed in these virtues, and thereby brought on the fall of the race in Adam, so Mary by means of the same had a part in its restoration. . . . [They] declare that she was *not* a mere instrument in the Incarnation . . . they declare she co-operated in our salvation not merely by the descent of the Holy Ghost upon her body, but by specific holy acts, the effect of the Holy Ghost within her soul; that, as Eve forfeited privileges by sin, so Mary earned privileges by the fruits of grace; that, as Eve was disobedient and unbelieving, so Mary was obedient and believing; that, as Eve was a cause of ruin to all, Mary was a cause of salvation to all; that as Eve made room for Adam's fall, so Mary made room for our Lord's reparation of it; and thus, whereas the free gift was not as the offence, but much greater, it follows that, as Eve co-operated in effecting a greater evil, Mary co-operated in effecting a much greater good.[13]

The disagreement between Catholics and Protestants with regard to Mary lies essentially in this difference: Catholics regard her as an active agent in our redemption, whereas Protestants see her as merely the more or less passive means to redemption. The divergence is partly the result of different theologies of grace.

> If Eve was raised above human nature by that indwelling moral gift which we call grace, is it rash to say that Mary had even a greater grace? And this consideration gives significance to the Angel's salutation of her as "full of grace,"—an interpretation of the original word which is undoubtedly the right one, as soon as we resist the common Protestant assumption that grace is a mere external approbation or acceptance, answering to the word "favour," whereas it is, as the Fathers teach, a real inward condition or superadded quality of soul.[14]

It is the Catholic idea of grace that makes the doctrine of the immaculate conception meaningful and, given that Mary is the second Eve, inevitable. For, "if Eve had this supernatural inward gift given her from the first moment of her personal existence, is it possible to deny that Mary too had this gift from the very first moment of her personal existence?" And, Newman concludes, "this is simply and literally the doctrine of the Immaculate Conception." Provided one believes in "the supernatural endowment of our first parents," it is not difficult to believe that Mary had "a superadded fulness of grace, and that from the first moment of her existence." If Eve had not fallen, her children would in turn have received "what may be called an immaculate conception." And so one may call Mary, "as it were, a daughter of Eve unfallen."

But one can only understand what it means to say that Mary was conceived without original sin, if one grasps that in Catholic theology original sin is not sin in the usual sense of the word. Newman explains that original sin

> is a term denoting Adam's sin as transferred to us, or the state to which Adam's sin reduces his children; but by Protestants it seems to be understood as sin, in much the same sense as actual sin. We, with the Fathers, think of it as something negative, Protestants as something positive. Protestants hold that it is a disease, a radical change of nature, an active poison internally corrupting the soul,

infecting its primary elements, and disorganizing it; and they fancy that we ascribe a different nature from ours to the Blessed Virgin,
different from that of her parents, and from that of fallen Adam.
We hold nothing of the kind; we consider that in Adam she died,
as others; that she was included, together with the whole race,
in Adam's sentence; that she incurred his debt, as we do; but that,
for the sake of Him who was to redeem her and us upon the Cross,
to her the debt was remitted by anticipation, on her the sentence
was not carried out, except indeed as regards her natural death,
for she died when her time came, as others. All this we teach,
but we deny that she had original sin; for by original sin we mean
. . . something negative . . . the *deprivation* of that supernatural
unmerited grace which Adam and Eve had on their first formation,—deprivation and the consequences of deprivation. Mary
could not merit, any more than they, the restoration of that grace;
but it was restored to her by God's free bounty, from the very first
moment of her existence, and thereby, in fact, she never came
under the original curse, which consisted in the loss of it. And
she had this special privilege, in order to fit her to become the
Mother of her and our Redeemer, to fit her mentally, spiritually
for it; so that, by the aid of the first grace, she might so grow in
grace, that, when the Angel came and her Lord was at hand, she
might be "full of grace," prepared as far as a creature could be
prepared, to receive Him into her bosom.

With regard to the objection of medieval theologians like St.
Thomas Aquinas that Mary could hardly have been redeemed
if she was not a sinner, Newman replies that the doctrine would
never have been opposed if it had been made clear that "the
doctrine meant nothing else than that in fact in her case the
general sentence on mankind was not carried out, and that,
by means of the indwelling in her of divine grace from the first
moment of her being."[15]

Newman has less to say about the (as yet undefined) doctrine of the assumption, but he does point to the vision of the
woman and the child in the book of Revelation. He admits that
it may be objected first that "such an interpretation is but poorly

supported by the Fathers, and secondly that in ascribing such a picture of the Madonna (as it may be called) to the Apostolic age, I am committing an anachronism." To the first objection he replies that "Christians have never gone to Scripture for proof of their doctrines, till there was actual need, from the pressure of controversy." The second objection he refuses to allow:

> The Virgin and Child is *not* a mere modern idea; on the contrary, it is represented again and again . . . in the paintings of the Catacombs. Mary is there drawn with the Divine Infant in her lap, she with hands extended in prayer, He with His hand in the attitude of blessing. No representation can more forcibly convey the doctrine of the high dignity of the Mother, and . . . of her influence with her Son. Why should the memory of His time of subjection be so dear to Christians, and so carefully preserved?[16]

In interpreting the passage in the twelfth chapter of Revelation, which is the scriptural basis of the doctrine of the assumption, Newman agrees that "under the image of the Woman, the Church is signified; but what I would maintain is this, that the Holy Apostle would not have spoken of the Church under this particular image, *unless* there had existed a blessed Virgin Mary, who was exalted on high, and the object of veneration to all the faithful." Just as the woman in the vision clearly represents the Church, so "the Child represents the children of the Church." This "is the real or direct sense," but "what is the sense of the symbol under which that real sense is conveyed? *who* are the Woman and the Child? I answer, they are not personifications but Persons. This is true of the Child, therefore it is true of the Woman." Again,

> not only Mother and Child, but a serpent is introduced into the vision. Such a meeting of man, woman, and serpent has not been found in Scripture, since the beginning of Scripture, and now it is found in its end. Moreover, in the passage in the Apocalypse as if to supply, before Scripture came to an end, what was wanting in its beginning, we are told, and for the first time, that the serpent in Paradise was the evil spirit.

Newman also points out in an important observation on the literary form of the Bible that

> the image of the woman, according to general Scripture usage, is too bold and prominent for a mere personification. Scripture is not fond of allegories. We have indeed frequent figures there, as when the sacred writers speak of the arm or sword of the Lord . . . or of the Church as a bride or as a vine; but they are not much given to dressing up abstract ideas or generalizations in personal attributes.[17]

Newman concludes that Mary's immaculate conception and assumption, "her sanctity and her greatness," should be no surprise when we consider that Mary is the Mother of God, not in any merely rhetorical sense, but in "a well-weighed, grave, dogmatic sense, which corresponds and is adequate to its sound. It intends to express that God is her Son, as truly as any one of us is the son of his own mother." This "awful title" is both "the issue of her sanctity" and "the origin of her greatness."[18]

Given the Catholic doctrine about Mary, Marian devotion follows as a matter of course:

> I conceive it impossible . . . for those who believe the Church to be one vast body in heaven and on earth, in which every holy creature of God has its place, and of which prayer is the life, when once they recognize the sanctity and dignity of the Blessed Virgin, not to perceive immediately, that her office above is one of perpetual intercession for the faithful militant, and that our very relation to her must be that of clients to a patron, and that, in the eternal enmity which exists between the woman and the serpent, while the serpent's strength lies in being the Tempter, the weapon of the Second Eve and Mother of God is prayer.

It is not necessary to believe that Mary should hear our prayers

> by any innate power, or any personal gift; but by His manifestation to her of the prayers which we make to her. When Moses was on the Mount, the Almighty told him of the idolatry of his people at the foot of it, in order that he might intercede for them;

and thus it is the Divine Presence which is the intermediating Power by which we reach her and she reaches us.[19]

But Newman emphasizes that "intercession is one thing, devotion is another." We do not have to invoke Mary for her to intercede for us; otherwise Protestants, not to mention early Christians, would be deprived of her intercession:

> Our Lord died for those heathens who did not know Him; and His Mother intercedes for those Christians who do not know her; and she intercedes according to His will, and, when He wills to save a particular soul, she at once prays for it. I say, He wills indeed according to her prayer, but then she prays according to His will.[20]

Far from devotion to Mary interfering with our worship of Jesus Christ, Newman claims that "just those nations and countries have lost their faith in the divinity of Christ, who have given up devotion to His Mother, and that those on the other hand, who had been foremost in her honour, have retained their orthodoxy." And he concludes with memorable succinctness: "In the Catholic Church Mary has shown herself, not the rival, but the minister of her Son; she has protected Him, as in His infancy, so in the whole history of the Religion."[21]

5
CHURCH

The Visible Church

Newman's Anglican preaching contains many references to the Church. The idea of an independent or free-lance Christian is dismissed simply on the moral ground that a person who "stands forth *on his own ground*, declaring himself as an individual a witness for Christ," would be "grieving and disturbing the calm spirit given us by God," whereas we are called to "unite together in one, and to shelter our personal profession under the authority of the general body," thus removing "from us individually the burden of a high profession, of implying great things of ourselves by inventing for ourselves solemn prayers and praises."[1] Against the prevailing Protestant idea that doctrine is derived from the Bible, Newman insists in a sermon dating from 1833, the first year of the Tractarian movement: "Christ has so willed it, that we should get at the Truth, not by ingenious speculations, reasonings, or investigations of our own, but by teaching. The Holy Church has been set up from the beginning as a solemn religious fact . . . as a picture, a revelation of the next world, as itself the Christian Dispensation."[2]

It is hard to imagine a "higher" view of the Church than one in which the Church and Christianity are synonymous. Instead of an invisible religion, Newman stresses that the Church "is a visible body, and, to appearance, an institution

73

of this world."[3] It is a "Kingdom which Christ has set up"—or
rather, "a new kingdom has been established, not merely
different from all kingdoms before it, but contrary to them; a
paradox in the eyes of man,—the visible rule of the invisible
Saviour."[4] How was this done? After all, the gospel could simply
have been "left to the world at large" to accept or reject, once
it had been "recorded . . . in the Bible." But this was not the
case, Newman insists.

> Christ formed a body; He secured that body from dissolution by
> the bond of a Sacrament. He committed the privileges of His
> spiritual kingdom and the maintenance of His faith as a legacy
> to this baptized society . . . . Christianity has not been spread,
> as other systems, in an isolated manner, or by books; but from a
> centre, by regularly formed bodies, descendants of the three thou-
> sand, who, after St. Peter's preaching on the day of Pentecost,
> joined themselves to the Apostles' doctrine and fellowship.[5]

Rejecting any notion of an "Invisible Church . . . as if Scriptures said one word, anywhere, of a spiritual body existing in
this world separate from, and independent of, the Visible
Church," Newman allows that "no harm can come of the distinction of the Church into Visible and Invisible, while we view
it as, on the whole, but one in different aspects; as Visible,
because consisting (for instance) of clergy and laity—as Invisible, because resting for its life and strength upon unseen in-
fluences and gifts from Heaven." In fact, the New Testament
tells us that the Church "is a visible body, invested with, or . . .
existing in invisible privileges," for "the Church would cease
to be the Church, did the Holy Spirit leave it," since "its outward rites and forms are nourished and animated by the living
power which dwells within it."[6] Indeed, the Church is the Holy
Spirit's "especial dwelling-place."[7] For while Christ came "to
die for us; the Spirit came to make us one in Him who had
died and was alive, that is, to form the Church." The Church,
then, is "the one mystical body of Christ . . . quickened by
the Spirit"—and it is "one" by virtue of the Holy Spirit "giving
it *life*."[8]

Because Scripture, the Fathers, and the early Church all witnessed to the oneness of the Church, the Tractarian Newman was obliged to embrace the so-called branch theory: whereas there had once been "but one vast body of Christians, called the Church, throughout the world," now that "vast Catholic body" was "broken into many fragments." Nevertheless, he remained acutely aware of a unity that was not merely an ideal but had once existed, not for any human organizational reasons but because Christ actually "constituted one Holy Society."[9] Again, as an Anglican he recognized the importance of the Petrine office for the unity of the Church: "In St. Peter . . . the rock on which the Church is founded, we see, as in a type, its unity, stability, and permanence. It is set up in one name, not in many, to show that it is one; and that name is Peter."[10] What Newman calls "Gospel privileges" are connected

> with the circumstance or condition of unity in those who receive them; the image of Christ and token of their acceptance being stamped upon them *then*, at that moment, when they are considered as *one*; so that henceforth the whole multitude, no longer viewed as mere individual men, become portions or members of the indivisible Body of Christ Mystical, so knit together in Him by Divine Grace, that all have what He has, and each has what all have.[11]

Already, then, as an Anglican Newman had accepted the Catholic belief that the oneness or unity of the Church is not merely a desirable ecclesiastical state of affairs but an essential note of the Church. He saw that this followed from the way Christ had founded the Church—or rather from his twofold foundation. For, when Christ

> came as a Spirit, and, so coming, did for His own that which the visible flesh and blood of the Son of man, from its very nature, could not do, viz., He came into the souls of all who believe, and taking possession of them, He, being One, knit them altogether into one. Christ, by coming in the flesh, provided an external or apparent unity, such as had been under the Law. He formed His

Apostles into a visible society; but when He came again in the Person of His Spirit, He made them all in a real sense one, not in name only. For they were no longer arranged merely in the form of unity, as the limbs of the dead may be, but they were parts and organs of one unseen power; they really depended upon, and were offshoots of that which was One.[12]

In other words, the oneness of the Church arises not out of the need for institutional cohesion or even fraternal union but out of the unity of the Triune God.

Although Newman's patristic conception of the inner nature of the Church belongs more to the mystical theology of the Eastern Church than to the more juridical ecclesiology of the Latin, or at least Tridentine, Church, he is by no means without a very strong sense of the external institutional reality of the Church. For humanly speaking, the Church "is a visible body, and, to appearance, an institution of this world."[13] Since, therefore, "Christ has set up a kingdom in the world," "a counter kingdom" to the "kingdoms of this world,"[14] this kingdom is far from being only a spiritual one, even while ultimately it depends on the Spirit for its existence. Indeed, Newman declares, "It is as unmeaning to speak of an invisible kingdom on earth, as of invisible chariots and horsemen, invisible swords and spears, invisible palaces; to be a kingdom at all it must be visible, if the word has any true meaning."[15] Preaching again as an Anglican, he argues that Scripture speaks of "the visible appearance and display of . . . one kingdom in all lands."[16] Almost as though issuing a challenge to those modern Catholic theologians who, in reaction to an excessively juridical ecclesiology, anxiously minimize as far as possible the hierarchical institution, Newman takes an unequivocal stand based on Scripture:

> If we will be scriptural in our view of the Church, we must consider that it is a kingdom, that its officers have great powers and high gifts, that they are charged with the custody of Divine Truth, that they are all united together, and that the nations are subject

to them. If we reject this kind of ministry, as inapplicable to the present day, we shall in vain go to Scripture to find another.

If the Gospels clearly indicate "the imperial nature of Christ's kingdom, much more is this peculiarity of it drawn out in the prophetical writings" of the Old Testament.[17] "Has there not," asks Newman rhetorically, "in fact, been a great corporation, or continuous body politic, all over the world, from the Apostles' days to our own, bearing the name of Church—one, and one only?"[18] And it is this Church which has obtained that "universal dominion, or Catholicity" which "all empires of this world have sought after."[19] Unfortunately for the Anglican preacher, this "Kingdom of Christ" is no longer "at unity with itself" but is now "broken up into sections."[20]

Closely linked to the unity and oneness of the Church is its catholicity or universality. This, says Newman, is "its great note" that

> it is Catholic, universal every where; and this note is insisted on as something special in itself, of a nature to dazzle and subdue the mind, like a miracle, or like the sun's light in the heavens. It was to be the characteristic gift of the Christian Church, that she herself was to be a great public evidence of her mission, that she was to be her own evidence. Her very look, her bearing, her voice were to be her credentials.[21]

So wrote the Anglican Newman. As a Catholic, he noted the paradox of having had to hold that "the Church was one indeed, and the Church was Catholic indeed, but that the one Church was not the Catholic, and the Catholic Church was not the one"; he pointed out that the "one Church" is necessarily "Catholic, because it embraces all Christians at once in one extended whole, its catholicity being coincident with its unity." This "external unity," itself "emphatically" a sacrament of unity, contains "the transmission and warrant of Divine privilege,"[22] and, "as it is the divinely blessed symbol and pledge of the true faith, so also it is the obvious means . . . of securing it."[23] The Church, of course, also has the note of apostolicity insofar as she teaches "the doctrine of the Apostles" and possesses "the Apostolical ministry."[24]

The Corruption of the Church

The Creed proclaims belief in One, Holy, Catholic, and Apostolic Church. And so the Church also possesses what Newman once as an Anglican called "the great Note of the Church," namely sanctity.[25] But if holiness is an essential mark of the Church, then how is it that sin seems also to be a distinctly marked characteristic as well? The difficulty led Newman to develop a veritable theology of the corruption of the Church, and indeed his thinking on this subject was a central factor in his conversion to Roman Catholicism. It is a problem which still disturbs many people, not the least of them Roman Catholics. The simplest answer is to point to the foundation of the Church in the New Testament, or rather to the Gospels. "Even among the Apostles themselves, one was a 'Devil,'" remarks Newman: "No wonder then that ever since, whether among the rulers or the subjects of the Church, sin has abounded."[26] But in a much less dramatic way the Church in its sinful human members cannot help but seem sinful, and more sinful than holy:

> Even supposing there were a society of men influenced individually by Christian motives, still this society, viewed as a whole, would be a worldly one; I mean a society holding and maintaining many errors, and countenancing many bad practices. Evil ever floats at the top. And if we inquire why it is that the good in Christians is seen less than the bad? I answer, first, because there is less of it; and secondly, because evil forces itself upon general notice, and good does not.

And so, Newman argues, there is an important sense in which the real holiness of the Church is hidden from view:

It is only the actions of others which we see for the most part . . . God only sees the circumstances under which a man acts, and why he acts in this way and not in that. God only sees perfectly the train of thought which preceded his action, the motive, and the reasons. . . . Think for a moment, how many hours in the day every man is left wholly to himself and his God, or rather how few minutes he is in intercourse with others—consider this, and you will perceive how it is that the life of the Church is hid with God, and how it is that the outward conduct of the Church must necessarily look like the world, even far more than it really is like it.

There are words of warning against judging people by their outward behavior, which ought to make us more cautious in our criticisms of the Church, especially perhaps of its leaders:

Consider, moreover, how much there is, while we are in the body, to stand in the way of one mind communicating with another. We are imprisoned in the body, and our intercourse is by means of words, which feebly represent our real feelings. Hence the best motives and truest opinions are misunderstood.[27]

However, genuine corruptions in the Church should be no surprise as they were clearly predicted by Christ himself in the Gospels. In Newman's earlier Protestant years as an Anglican, he thought that such prophecies had been visibly fulfilled in the corruptions particularly of the papacy. Later, as a Catholic, he came to see these same corruptions not as evidence that the Church of Rome was the Church of the Antichrist but rather almost as notes of the true Church! For corruption is now seen as inseparable from a living Church: "Things that do not admit of abuse have very little life in them."[28] And it is this very quality of "life" which Newman insists on as an especial note of the Church: "The Church is emphatically a living body . . . she alone revives even if she declines; heretical and schismatical bodies cannot keep life."[29]

Not only did Christ predict scandals, but in the parable of the tares and the wheat, for example, he spoke of the Church "as in its very constitution made up of good and bad." The corruption of the Church has existed from the time of Judas Iscariot and indeed is so "bound up with the very idea of Christianity" as to be "almost a dogma."[30] Given that the world is sinful, once "it has poured into the Church, it has insulted and blasphemed the religion which it professed, in a special way, in which heathenism cannot insult it." One would expect, Newman adds, to find greater corruption in the Catholic Church than in a Protestant Church, for "a Protestant world cannot commit that sin which a Catholic world can." When ordinary human weaknesses are "coupled with that intense absolute faith which Catholics have, and Protestants have not," one finds "acts of inconsistency, of superstition, violence etc which are not to be looked for external to the Catholic Church."[31] In other words, on the old principle that the corruption of the best is the worst, if the claims of the Catholic Church are anything to go by, one would expect to find in it the greatest scandals. In particular, in regard to the papacy, "where you have power, you will have the abuse of power—and the more absolute, the stronger, the more sacred the power, the greater and more certain will be its abuse."[32] Because, too, the Church is a visible polity, it is also "necessarily a political power, and to touch politics is to touch pitch."[33]

Towards the end of his life, in the great 1877 Preface to the *Via Media*, Newman tackled the sensitive problem of corruption in a more profoundly theological manner. The Church, he points out, is the mystical body of Christ, who "is Prophet, Priest, and King; and after His pattern, and in human measure, Holy Church has a triple office too; not the Prophetical alone and in isolation . . . but three offices, which are indivisible, though diverse, viz. teaching, rule, and sacred ministry." It follows that Christianity "is at once a philosophy, a political power, and a religious rite: as a religion, it is Holy; as a philosophy, it is Apostolic; as a political power, it is imperial, that is, One and Catholic. As a religion, its special centre of action is pastor and flock; as a philosophy, the Schools; as a rule, the Papacy and its Curia." These three different offices are based on different principles, use different means, and are liable to different corruptions:

> Truth is the guiding principle of theology and theological inquiries; devotion and edification, of worship; and of government, expedience. The instrument of theology is reasoning; of worship, our emotional nature; of rule, command and coercion. Further, in man as he is, reasoning tends to rationalism; devotion to superstition and enthusiasm; and power to ambition and tyranny.

The difficulty of combining all three offices is well illustrated by the question, "What line of conduct, except on the long, the very long run, is at once edifying, expedient, and true?" Certainly, the charism of infallibility protects the Catholic Church from error not only directly in teaching but also "indirectly" in "worship and political action also"; however, "nothing but the gift of impeccability granted to her authorities would secure them from all liability to mistake in their conduct, policy, words and decisions." The problem of exercising these three very different functions "supplies the staple of those energetic charges and vivid pictures of the inconsistency, double-dealing, and deceit of the Church of Rome."

Far from blaming the corruptions to be found in the Church on Catholic theology, as he had done as an Anglican, he now observes that "ambition, craft, cruelty, and superstition are not commonly the characteristic of theologians," whereas the alleged corruptions in fact "bear on their face the marks of having a popular or a political origin," and "theology, so far from encouraging them, has restrained and corrected such extravagances as have been committed, through human infirmity, in the exercise of the regal and sacerdotal powers." Indeed, he adds dramatically, religion is never "in greater trouble than when, in consequence of national or international troubles, the Schools of theology have been broken up and ceased to be." He then gives the reason for this in some of the weightiest words he ever wrote:

I say, then, Theology is the fundamental and regulating principle of the whole Church system. It is commensurate with Revelation, and Revelation is the initial and essential idea of Christianity. It is the subject-matter, the formal cause, the expression, of the Prophetical Office, and, as being such, has created both the Regal Office and the Sacerdotal. And it has in a certain sense a power of jurisdiction over those offices, as being its own creations, theologians being ever in request and in employment in keeping within bounds both the political and popular elements in the Church's constitution,—elements which are far more congenial than itself to the human mind, are far more liable to excess and corruption. . . . [34]

A charge often leveled at the Catholic Church is that of the corruption of its worship, in other words of superstition. But Newman argues that the kind of popular religion likely to cause scandal may be traced to the gospel itself, and he cites the example of the woman with the hemorrhage who hoped to be cured by touching the cloak of Jesus, who "passed over the superstitious act" and healed her because of her faith. In fact, he praised her for "what might, not without reason, be called an idolatrous act." Actually the Gospels show that the "idolatry of ignorance" is not regarded on a level with other idolatries (of wealth, for example), which, however, are not normally "shocking to educated minds." Jesus constantly insisted on the necessity of faith—"but where does He insist on the danger of superstition?" However, the fact remains that this and other incidents in the Gospels "form an aspect of Apostolic Christianity very different from that presented" by the Epistles of St. Paul. "Need men wait for the Medieval Church in order to make their complaint that the theology of Christianity does not accord with its religious manifestations?" Does "a poor Neapolitan crone, who chatters to the crucifix" do anything inherently more superstitious than the woman with the hemorrhage? Given "the ethical intelligence of the world at large," Newman would wonder "whether that nation really had the faith, which is free in all its ranks and classes from all kinds and degrees of what is commonly considered superstition."

There is no reason to be surprised if the Catholic Church, in the face of popular religion, finds it difficult "to make her Sacerdotal office keep step with her Prophetical." This applies obviously to the cult of the angels and saints, which, "though ever to be watched with jealousy by theologians, because of human infirmity and perverseness . . . has a normal place in revealed Religion." For monotheism implies beings who are inferior to God but superior to human beings, and who are able to bridge "the vast gulf which separates Him from man." And so polytheism is only "a natural sentiment corrupted." The Church's mission is not "to oppose herself to impulses" that are "both natural and legitimate," though previously "the instruments of sin, but to do her best, by a right use, to moderate and purify them." The fact that the Church has not always been successful simply shows that "there will ever be a marked contrariety between the professions of her theology and the ways and doings of a Catholic country."[35]

The Laity

As an Anglican, Newman was clear that salvation is not a simply individual affair: we are saved through the Church. We "come to Christ in faith, through the Church." This formula encapsulates both the need for personal faith and the necessity of membership of the Body of Christ. Evangelical Christians may see a contradiction—but "were a person to say that he would give some benefit, food or clothing, to any poor person who wanted it, would any one say that he broke his promise, if he appointed some particular place where the food or the clothing were to be got, and where those who desired it must go for it?" However, just as later as a Roman Catholic he is quite prepared to allow that salvation is possible outside the Church, so now he maintains that "it is a great comfort to believe that God's favour is not limited to the bounds of His heritage, but that, in the Church or out of the Church, every one that calleth on the Name of the Lord with a pure and perfect heart shall be saved."[36]

This is not the place to tell the story of Newman's conversion to the Roman Catholic Church. The only point that needs to be emphasized here is that it was not primarily a question of "authority" for him as it was for many other converts of his time and since; nor was it fundamentally a question of disillusionment with the Church of England. The real issue for Newman was whether or not the Church of Rome in the nineteenth century was the same Church as that of the first centuries and the Fathers, whether contemporary Catholicism was essentially the same religion as early Christianity. It was, in fact, a profoundly ecclesiological problem.

Although as a convert Newman was anxious to avoid becoming involved in strictly theological issues, he was soon drawn not only into controversy but also gradually into developing a theology of the Church. The resulting ecclesiology is the great theological work of his Catholic period. His early awareness of the failure, or rather refusal, of the authorities to allow the laity the kind of participation in the Church's life that was possible in the Church of England eventually led him to write his celebrated article "On Consulting the Faithful in Matters of Doctrine" (1859). The immediate cause of the essay was a sharp attack by a seminary professor on some lines Newman had written in the controversial journal the *Rambler*, in which he declared boldly that the bishops should

> really desire to know the opinion of the laity on subjects in which the laity are especially concerned. If even in the preparation of a dogmatic definition the faithful are consulted, as lately in the instance of the Immaculate Conception, it is at least as natural to anticipate such an act of kind feeling and sympathy in great practical questions.

And he added for good measure a general warning against "the misery of any division between the rulers of the Church and the educated laity."[37]

As a result of this incident, Newman determined to deal more fully with the place of the laity in the Church. In "On Consulting the Faithful in Matters of Doctrine," which was also published in the *Rambler*, he begins by defending his use of the word *consult*, which he says in ordinary English "includes the idea of inquiring into a matter of *fact*, as well as asking a judgment." Thus, for example, a "physician consults the pulse of his patient; but not in the same sense in which his patient consults *him*." It is in the former sense that the Church "consults" or "regards" the faith of the laity before defining a doctrine. The *Rambler* was written for lay people, not for scholastic theologians, to whom the word *consult* would naturally signify its Latin sense of "consult *with*." But if the laity's "advice, their opinion, their judgment on the question of definition is not asked," nevertheless, "the matter of fact, viz. their belief, *is* sought for, as a testimony to that apostolical tradition, on which alone any doctrine whatsoever can be defined." Newman balances his criticism of scholastic orthodoxy by rejecting the suggestion that he is

> comparing such precision (far from it) with that true religious zeal which leads theologians to keep the sacred Ark of the Covenant in every letter of its dogma, as a tremendous deposit for which they are responsible. In this curious sceptical world, such sensitiveness is the only human means by which the treasure of faith can be kept inviolate. There is a woe in Scripture against the unfaithful shepherd. We do not blame the watch-dog because he sometimes flies at the wrong person. I conceive the force, the peremptoriness, the sternness, with which the Holy See comes down upon the vagrant or the robber, trespassing upon the enclosure of revealed truth, is the only sufficient antagonist to the power and subtlety of the world, to imperial comprehensiveness, monarchical selfishness, nationalism, the liberalism of philosophy, the encroachments and usurpation of science.[38]

Having defended his use of the word *consult*, he now turns to consider the question, why consult the laity? The answer is plain, he says: "because the body of the faithful is one of the witnesses to the fact of the tradition of revealed doctrine, and because their *consensus* through Christendom is the voice of the Infallible Church." There are "channels of tradition," through which "the tradition of the Apostles, committed to the whole Church . . . manifests itself variously at various times," none of which "may be treated with disrespect," even though the hierarchy has sole responsibility for "discerning, discriminating, defining, promulgating, and enforcing any portion of that tradition." He himself, he explains, is "accustomed to lay great stress on the *consensus fidelium*" in order to compensate for the lack of testimony from bishops and theologians in favor of defined points of doctrine. At the time of the definition of the immaculate conception, his own bishop had referred to the faith of the laity as a "reflection" of the teaching of the Church, and Newman comments with dry irony: "Reflection; that is, the people are a *mirror*, in which the Bishops see themselves. Well, I suppose a person may *consult* his glass, and in that way may know things about himself which he can learn in no other way."[39]

He now proceeds to his celebrated historical example drawn from that period of the early Church's history which he had studied so deeply and intensely as an Anglican. In spite of the fact that the fourth century was the age of great doctors and saints who were also bishops (Athanasius, Ambrose, Chrysostom, and Augustine, for example), "nevertheless in that very day the divine tradition committed to the infallible Church was proclaimed and maintained far more by the faithful than by the Episcopate." During the Arian heresy, "in that time of immense confusion the divine dogma of our Lord's divinity was proclaimed, enforced, maintained, and (humanly speaking) preserved, far more by the 'Ecclesia docta' than by the 'Ecclesia docens' . . . the body of the episcopate was unfaithful to its commission, while the body of the laity was faithful to its baptism." The importance of the illustration is shown by the fact that it occurred so early in the history of the Church and involved the very identity of Christ. Newman boldly concludes by saying that "there was a temporary suspense of the functions" of the teaching Church, the unpalatable truth being that the "body of Bishops failed in their confession of the faith." The danger of the present time, when the hierarchy was so faithful and orthodox, was that the role of the laity would be neglected—but "each constituent portion of the Church has its proper functions, and no portion can safely be neglected." The article ends with the warning:

> I think certainly that the *Ecclesia docens* is more happy when she has . . . enthusiastic partisans about her . . . than when she cuts off the faithful from the study of her divine doctrines . . . and requires from them a *fides implicita* in her word, which in the educated classes will terminate in indifference, and in the poorer in superstition.[40]

Authority and Freedom

Newman's concern about the clericalization of the Church and the downgrading of the laity was equalled by his dismay at the growing authoritarianism in nineteenth-century Catholicism which reached its apogee with a concerted clamor for the definition of papal infallibility. Just as Newman championed the rights of the laity, so too he defended a responsible freedom in theological investigation and inquiry against the excesses of the so-called Ultramontanes. In one of his finest writings, the last chapter of the *Apologia*, he offers a careful and subtle exploration of the relation between theologians and the magisterium.

Newman's starting point is a defense of the infallibility of the Church. Granted that "truth is the real object of our reason," then "right reason" when "correctly exercised" arrives at religious truth. But unfortunately, "reason as it acts in fact and concretely in fallen man" has a "tendency . . . towards a simple unbelief," and there is no denying "the all-corroding, all-dissolving scepticism of the intellect," which has resulted in an "anarchical condition of things." Just as "in the pagan world, when our Lord came, the last traces of the religious knowledge of former times were all but disappearing from those portions of the world in which the intellect had been active and had had a career," so too, in the modern world, "What a scene, what a prospect, does the whole of Europe present at this day!" The necessity "to arrest fierce wilful human nature in its onward course" in order to preserve "some form of religion for the interests of humanity" led to the establishment of religion at the Reformation in Protestant countries, "but now the crevices of those establishments are admitting the enemy"; nor can the Bible as "a book . . . make a stand against the wild living intellect of man." The conflict between the claims of reason and religion is resolved through "the Church's infallibility, as a provision, adapted by the mercy of the Creator, to preserve religion in the world, and to restrain that freedom of thought, which of course in itself is one of the greatest of our natural gifts, and to rescue it from its own suicidal excesses." This "power . . . is happily adapted to be a working instrument . . . for smiting hard and throwing back the immense energy of the aggressive, capricious, untrustworthy intellect."[41]

There follows a severely uncompromising exposition of the Church's authority "viewed in its fulness" and "viewed in the concrete, as clothed and surrounded by the appendages of its high sovereignty . . . a supereminent prodigious power sent upon earth to encounter and master a giant evil." Although infallibility strictly only belongs to solemn dogmatic definitions, Newman professes to submit not only to the traditions of the Church, but also "to those other decisions of the Holy See, theological or not . . . which, waiving the question of their infallibility, on the lowest ground come to me with a claim to be accepted and obeyed." Nor does he feel any "temptation at all to break in pieces the great legacy of thought" which the Church has inherited from its greatest thinkers. This raises the obvious objection that "the restless intellect of our common humanity is utterly weighed down" by such an authority, "so that, if this is to be the mode of bringing it into order, it is brought into order only to be destroyed." Newman's reply is that in fact the "energy of the human intellect . . . thrives and is joyous, with a tough elastic strength, under the terrible blows of the divinely-fashioned weapon, and is never so much itself as when it has lately been overthrown." And he argues that far from being mutually contradictory, authority and reason need each other precisely because, paradoxically, each is actually sustained by conflict with the other:

> It is the vast Catholic body itself, and it only, which affords an arena for both combatants in that awful, never-dying duel. It is necessary for the very life of religion . . . that the warfare should be incessantly carried on. Every exercise of Infallibility is brought out into act by an intense and varied operation of the Reason, both as its ally and as its opponent, and provokes again, when it has done its work, a re-action of Reason against it; and, as in a civil polity the State exists and endures by means of the rivalry and collision, the encroachments and defeats of its constituent parts, so in like manner Catholic Christendom is no simple exhibition of religious absolutism, but presents a continuous picture of Authority and Private Judgment alternately advancing and retreating as the ebb and flow of the tide;—it is a vast assemblage of human beings with wilful intellects and wild passions, brought together into one by the beauty and the Majesty of a Superhuman Power,—into what may be called a large reformatory or training-school, not as if into a hospital or into a prison, not in order to be sent to bed, not to be buried alive, but (if I may change my metaphor) brought together as if into some moral factory, for the melting, refining, and moulding, by an incessant, noisy process, of the raw material of human nature, so excellent, so dangerous, so capable of divine purposes.[42]

The startling chain of imagery that concludes this richly metaphorical passage hints at a new, divergent movement of argument, and reminds us that Newman also has readers other than Protestants or unbelievers in mind. The infallible authority, he insists with a typically secular metaphor, "is a supply for a need, and it does not go beyond that need," for its purpose is "not to enfeeble the freedom or vigour of human thought in religious speculation, but to resist and control its extravagance."

Having begun by freely admitting the wide powers enjoyed by ecclesiastical authority, he now emphasizes both the narrow limits of infallibility in defining as explicit doctrine what is already implicit in revelation, and also its rare occurrence (normally by a "Pope in Ecumenical Council"). But, more important, he recognizes what "*is* the great trial to the Reason," namely, that the Church claims jurisdiction over a wide area of "secular matters which bear upon religion." These disciplinary rather than doctrinal judgments are not, however, infallible; nevertheless, they claim obedience (but not faith). Again, "because there is a gift of infallibility in the Catholic Church," it does not necessarily follow that "the parties who are in possession of it are in all their proceedings infallible." Indeed, "I think history supplies us with instances in the Church, where legitimate power has been harshly used." The unequivocal assertion of the Church's legitimate authority is thus sharply qualified by these reminders of its limits and restraints. But the apparent discrepancy is resolved by the consideration that it does not "follow that the substance of the acts of the ruling power is not right and expedient, because its manner may have been faulty." In fact, Newman remarks tartly, "high authorities act by means of instruments," and "we know how such instruments claim for themselves the name of their principals, who thus get the credit of faults which really are not theirs."[43]

The pages that follow are probably unrivaled in Newman's works for their sharply antithetical style of argument, brilliantly deployed to hold a carefully poised balance between two diametrically opposed points of view. But the object is not to play a balancing trick between conservative Catholics on the one side and liberal Catholics on the other. Nor is the pattern of thought no more than a rhetorical device designed to reach a compromise between the claims of both parties. For what emerges is that truth is attained not in spite of but through the conflict of opposites, which forces the crucial shift of perspective that allows the dilemma to be seen in a new light and so to be resolved.

Newman begins by reinforcing the case for authority and the

need for submission. Even Protestants "have before now obeyed the royal command to abstain from certain theological questions." Moreover, despite all abuses, Newman insists that ecclesiastical authority has been "mainly in the right, and that those whom they were hard upon were mainly in the wrong." For example, Origen "was wrong" and "his opponents were right." And yet "who can speak with patience of his enemy and the enemy of St. John Chrysostom, that Theophilus, bishop of Alexandria? who can admire or revere Pope Vigilius?" The contradiction is resolved by a completely fresh perspective, at once enlightening and provocative:

> In reading ecclesiastical history, when I was an Anglican, it used to be forcibly brought home to me, how the initial error of what afterwards became heresy was the urging forward of some truth against the prohibition of authority at an unseasonable time. There is a time for every thing, and many a man desires a reformation of an abuse, or the fuller development of a doctrine, or the adoption of a particular policy, but forgets to ask himself whether the right time for it is come: and knowing that there is no one who will be doing any thing towards its accomplishment in his own lifetime unless he does it himself, he will not listen to the voice of authority, and he spoils a good work in his own century, in order that another man, as yet unborn, may not have the opportunity of bringing it happily to perfection in the next. He may seem to the world to be nothing else than a bold champion for the truth and a martyr to free opinion, when he is just one of those persons whom the competent authority ought to silence; and, though the case may not fall within that subject-matter in which that authority is infallible, or the formal conditions of the exercise of that gift may be wanting, it is clearly the duty of authority to act vigorously in the case.

This, Newman admits, will arouse criticism, especially "if the ruling power happens in its proceedings to evince any defect of prudence or consideration." Mindful, no doubt, of his own difficulties with liberal Catholics who disliked his insistence on obedience, Newman adds that "all those who take the part of

that ruling authority will be considered as time-servers, or indifferent to the cause of uprightness and truth." But that is not
the conclusion of the sentence. The surprise, or rather the sting,
lies in the second half, directed not at the liberals, but at the
Ultramontanes: "while, on the other hand, the said authority
may be accidentally supported by a violent ultra party, which
exalts opinions into dogmas, and has it principally at heart to
destroy every school of thought but its own."

This "state of things" may well provoke and discourage people
of moderate views, as well as "such as keenly perceive, and are
honestly eager to remedy, existing evils"—"evils," Newman comments acidly, "of which divines in this or that foreign country
know nothing at all, and which even at home, where they exist, it is not every one who has the means of estimating." The
bewildering progress in modern knowledge raises the critical
question, "how are the respective claims of revelation and of
natural science to be adjusted?" particularly out of "tenderness
for those many souls who, in consequence of the confident tone
of the schools of secular knowledge, are in danger of being led
away into a bottomless liberalism of thought." This "deep, plau-
sible scepticism," which is "the development of human reason,
as practically exercised by the natural man," now constitutes
"the educated lay world." However, Newman is not intent on
attacking the "Liberal religionists of this day" ("a very mixed
body") or contemporary scientists and scholars, some of whom
may be hostile to religion, but many of whom pursue their
research in a completely disinterested spirit and should not be
blamed (as if one "were afraid of truth of any kind") for pursuing "secular facts, by means of the reason which God has given
them, to their logical conclusions." Rather, he is concerned for
those educated believers "who are simply perplexed,—frightened
or rendered desperate . . . by the utter confusion into which
late discoveries or speculations have thrown their most elemen-
tary ideas of religion."

Beneath the warm compassion runs a cold undercurrent of
contempt for the heartlessness of obscurantist dogmatism:

Who does not feel for such men? who can have one unkind thought of them? Let them be fierce with you who have no experience of the difficulty with which error is discriminated from truth, and the way of life is found amid the illusions of the world.

"How many a Catholic," exclaims Newman, "has in his thoughts followed such men, many of them so good, so true, so noble! how often has the wish risen in his heart that some one from among his own people should come forward as the champion of revealed truth against its opponents!" Indeed, he has himself been asked to do so by both Catholics and Protestants. But he raises a serious objection: "at the moment it is so difficult to say precisely what it is that is to be encountered and overthrown . . . hypotheses rise and fall." It is so "difficult to anticipate which of them will keep their ground" that "it has seemed to me to be very undignified for a Catholic to commit himself to the work of chasing what might turn out to be phantoms." Nor would such an attempt be likely to find favor with the authorities of the Church, whose "recent acts" may be interpreted, Newman suggests politely, as "tying the hands of a controversialist . . . and teaching us that true wisdom, which Moses inculcated on his people, when the Egyptians were pursuing them, 'Fear ye not, stand still; the Lord shall fight for you, and ye shall hold your peace.'" He concludes, therefore: "And so far from finding a difficulty in obeying in this case, I have cause to be thankful and to rejoice to have so clear a direction in a matter of difficulty."

In reality, Newman argues, there has never in the past been any conflict between religion and science. But immediately he qualifies the point both by admitting that it is too soon to pronounce on the relation between modern science and theology, and by freely conceding the one notorious exception to the rule, the case of Galileo. With this ambivalent allusion, the anti-Ultramontane undercurrent begins to swell to an undertow, stronger than the ostensible drift of the argument against objections to an infallible authority. The proof, Newman continues, that infallibility has not crushed intellectual freedom in the Church is that it is "individuals, and not the Holy See, that have taken the initiative, and given the lead to the Catholic mind, in theological inquiry." "Indeed," he points out, "it is one of the reproaches against the Roman Church, that it has originated nothing, and has only served as a sort of *remora* or break in the development of doctrine. And it is an objection which I really embrace as a truth; for such I conceive to be the main purpose of its extraordinary gift."

The historical examples that follow are unrelentingly negative. The fact is that "the Church of Rome possessed no great mind in the whole period of persecution." There was not a single Doctor till St. Leo, who anyway taught only "one point of doctrine." Not even Pope St. Gregory has a place in the history of theology. The greatest western theologian, St. Augustine, belonged, like the best early Latin theologians, to the African Church. Western theology, in fact, was formed to a considerable extent by heterodox theologians such as Tertullian and Origen and Eusebius, with the result that actual heretical "questionings" became "salutary truths." Even ecumenical councils were guided by the "individual reason" of a mere presbyter like Malchion, or a young deacon like Athanasius. At Trent, too, particular theologians "had a critical effect on some of the definitions of dogma." The real, albeit hidden, conclusion is that history gives little support to the Ultramontane view of Rome as a kind of oracle of truth.

History, too, shows how little authority has interfered with the freedom of theologians. But Newman is not only protesting against the present by means of the past; he is also stating with great deliberateness his considered view on the crucial balance to be maintained between theology and the teaching authority of the Church. He begins by referring (provocatively) to that medieval theocratic society so idealized by many of his contemporaries:

> There never was a time when the intellect of the educated class was more active, or rather more restless, than in the middle ages. And then again all through Church history from the first, how

slow is authority in interfering! Perhaps a local teacher, or a doctor in some local school, hazards a proposition, and a controversy
ensues. It smoulders or burns in one place, no one interposing;
Rome simply lets it alone. Then it comes before a Bishop; or some
priest, or some professor in some other seat of learning takes it
up; and then there is a second stage of it. Then it comes before
a University, and it may be condemned by the theological faculty. So the controversy proceeds year after year, and Rome is still
silent. An appeal perhaps is next made to a seat of authority inferior to Rome; and then at last after a long while it comes before
the supreme power. Meanwhile, the question has been ventilated
and turned over and over again, and viewed on every side of it,
and authority is called upon to pronounce a decision, which has
already been arrived at by reason. But even then, perhaps the
supreme authority hesitates to do so, and nothing is determined
on the point for years; or so generally and vaguely, that the whole
controversy has to be gone through again, before it is ultimately
determined.

Newman refrains from outright criticism of the abuse of
authority in the contemporary Church. But his point is clear
enough.

It is manifest how a mode of proceeding, such as this, tends not
only to the liberty, but to the courage, of the individual theologian
or controversialist. Many a man has ideas, which he hopes are true,
and useful for his day, but he is not confident about them, and
wishes to have them discussed. He is willing, or rather would be
thankful, to give them up, if they can be proved to be erroneous
or dangerous, and by means of controversy he achieves his end.
He is answered, and he yields; or on the contrary he finds that
he is considered safe. He would not dare to do this, if he knew
an authority, which was supreme and final, was watching every
word he said, and made signs of assent or dissent to each sentence,
as he uttered it. Then indeed he would be fighting, as the Persian
soldiers, under the lash, and the freedom of his intellect might
truly be said to be beaten out of him.

Nevertheless, he is ready to undermine his own indignation with the frank qualification that "when controversies run high" then "an interposition may . . . advisably take place; and again, questions may be of that urgent nature, that an appeal must, as a matter of duty, be made at once to the highest authority in the Church."

But the insistent emphasis on the universal character of the Church that follows barely conceals an unfavorable allusion to the Italian monopoly of the Holy See.

> The multitude of nations which are within the fold of the Church will be found to have acted for its protection, against any narrowness, on the supposition of narrowness, in the various authorities at Rome, with whom lies the practical decision of controverted questions. . . . Then, again, such national influences have a providential effect in moderating the bias which the local influences of Italy may exert on the See of St. Peter. It stands to reason that . . . Rome must have in it an element of Italy; and it is no prejudice to the zeal and devotion with which we submit ourselves to the Holy See to admit this plainly . . . Catholicity is not only one of the notes of the Church, but . . . one of its securities.

And the conclusion is uncompromising:

> I trust that all European races will ever have a place in the Church, and assuredly I think that the loss of the English, not to say the German element, in its composition has been a most serious misfortune. And certainly, if there is one consideration more than another which should make us English grateful to Pius the Ninth, it is that, by giving us a Church of our own, he has prepared the way for our own habits of mind, our own manner of reasoning, our own tastes, and our own virtues, finding a place and thereby a sanctification, in the Catholic Church.[44]

Since the Second Vatican Council, these hopes of Newman have, of course, been realized in the election of the first non-Italian Pope for several centuries, in the increasingly international character of the Roman curia, and in the new impor-

tance given to the local church. But while the council emphasized the importance of theologians, there are still many unresolved
problems concerning their relationship to the magisterium or
teaching authority of the Church. Newman's ecclesiology in
this area is valuable not only for the balance it strikes between
the interests of both sides, but also in two other respects. First,
his evenhanded approach still strikes a very original note in
its insistence on the positive fruits of a conflict that is as inevitable as it is potentially creative. Second, the mere fact that
Newman has no blueprint to offer to resolve these tensions is
itself significant in indicating that there are no simple solutions
to problems which no more admit of a theoretical answer than
does life itself.

Infallibility, Theology, and Conscience

Newman had no difficulty in accepting the First Vatican
Council's definition of papal infallibility, which was more
moderate and restrained than the kind of definition for which
the extreme Ultramontanes had been agitating. Before the actual definition was passed, he pointed out in a private letter
that however infallible the Pope might be, his pronouncements
would still require interpretation. The same was true of a council's definitions, which—just as "lawyers explain acts of Parliament"—had to be explained by theologians. Obvious as the fact
might be, the conclusion to be drawn from it had serious consequences for the fantasies of extreme Ultramontanism. "Hence,
I have never been able to see myself that the ultimate decision
rests with any but the general Catholic intelligence."[45] However,
later in A Letter to the Duke of Norfolk (1875) he was careful
to emphasize that he simply meant that the whole Church
ratified a definition as "authentic," not that the "subsequent
reception" actually entered into the "necessary conditions" of
a dogmatic decision.[46]

In the earlier private letter he also noted that abstract definitions could not "determine particular fact": the doctrine, for

example, that there was no salvation outside the Church did not apply to people in "invincible ignorance."[47] For "it does not follow, because there is no Church but one, which has the Evangelical gifts and privileges to bestow, that therefore no one can be saved without the intervention of that one Church." And it was "possible to belong to the soul of the Church without belonging to the body." Other teachings of the Church admitted of exceptions in practice, like the condemnations in theory of mixed education and usury. In the case of usury, moreover, as in that of the doctrine of absolute predestination, distinctions had been drawn between different connotations of the words in question, which had led to the serious modification, even suspension, of the abstract teaching. Such changes and qualifications in the Church's official teaching "show what caution is to be observed" in interpreting its pronouncements. But, on the other hand, because general doctrines cannot be divorced from concrete circumstances and contexts, it did not follow that condemnations of "the very wording" of particular doctrinal deviations in books may not be infallible, since otherwise "neither Pope nor Council could draw up a dogmatic definition at all, for the right exercise of words is involved in the right exercise of thought."[48]

He continued to insist after the definition that "the voice of the Schola Theologorum, of the whole Church diffusive" would "in time make itself heard," and that "Catholic instincts and ideas" would eventually "assimilate and harmonize" it into the wider context of Catholic belief.[49] As time went on, too, theologians would "settle the force of the wording of the dogma, just as the courts of law solve the meaning and bearing of Acts of Parliament."[50] It was hardly more than common sense that ultimately the solemn declarations of councils and popes could be authenticated only by the acceptance and recognition by the Church that the pronouncements were indeed what they purported to be; nevertheless, their interpretation involved necessarily the technicalities of theological science. The meaning of dogmatic statements was not self-evident, but they were "always made with the anticipation and condition of this lawyer-

like, or special-pleader-like, action of the intellect upon them."[51]
All human statements required interpretation. In defining doctrines, popes and councils enjoyed an "active infallibility," but
more was involved in the infallibility of the Church than that,
since a *"passive infallibility"* belonged to the whole Catholic
people, who had to determine the force and meaning of these
doctrinal definitions; the chief responsibility for this, however,
lay with the theologians, whose discussions and investigations
assured a clear distinction, essential for preventing "dogmatism,"
between "theological truth" and "theological opinion."
Differences between theologians maintained "liberty of thought,"
while their consensus on points of dogma was "the safeguard
of the infallible decisions of the Church."[52] Infallibility (itself
a comparatively recent term) resided in its fullness in the whole
Church (although this had always been assumed and never for-
mally defined).

Newman repeats and develops in *A Letter to the Duke of Norfolk* the points he had already made in private correspondence.
He does not hesitate to say that the "definite rules" and "traditional principles of interpretation" needed for explaining
dogmatic statements are "as cogent and unchangeable" as the
definitions themselves.[53] Central to this process, he claims, is
the "principle of minimizing,"[54] whereby theologians construe
"in the concrete" a pronouncement of the teaching authority,
"by strict interpretation of its wording, by the illustration of
its circumstances, and by the recognition of exceptions, in order
to make it as tolerable as possible, and the least of a temptation, to self-willed, independent, or wrongly educated minds."
After all, he insists, the virtue of faith is "so difficult," and "so
difficult is it to assent inwardly to propositions, verified to us
neither by reason nor experience, but depending for their reception on the word of the Church as God's oracle, that she has
ever shown the utmost care to contract, as far as possible, the
range of truths and the sense of propositions, of which she
demands this absolute reception."[55] This "legitimate minimizing" takes advantage on the one hand of the "intensely concrete character of the matters condemned" in "negative"

pronouncements, and on the other hand of the abstract nature of "affirmative" definitions of doctrine ("excepting such as relate to persons"), which "admit of exceptions in their actual application."[56] These principles have to be applied to the definition of papal infallibility, the scope of which is carefully limited to deliberate and actual definitions of faith and morals that are referable either to revelation or to the moral law, and that are intended to be authoritative teachings, binding on the whole Church as pertaining to salvation. In the event, however, of "a false interpretation" of the definition of infallibility, then "another Leo will be given us for the occasion." The reference is to Pope St. Leo's Council of Chalcedon, which, "without of course touching the definition" of the preceding Council of Ephesus, "trimmed the balance of doctrine by completing it."[57] The warning is an exact prophecy both of the theology of "creeping infallibility" that came in the wake of the First Vatican Council, and of the Second Vatican Council, which Pope John XXIII convoked nearly a hundred years later.

At the heart of A Letter to the Duke of Norfolk is the celebrated treatment of the sovereignty of conscience. Newman had often written on conscience as the basis of religious belief, but here he discusses the individual believer's conscience in its relation to legitimate ecclesiastical authority. He first defines conscience as the law of God "as apprehended in the minds of individual men"—which, "though it may suffer refraction in passing into the intellectual medium of each . . . is not therefore so affected as to lose its character of being the Divine Law, but still has, as such, the prerogative of commanding obedience." On this view, conscience is "the voice of God," whereas the world regards it as little more than "a creation of man." Far from being "a long-sighted selfishness" or "a desire to be consistent with oneself," Newman declares in ringing tones, "Conscience is the aboriginal Vicar of Christ, a prophet in its informations, a monarch in its peremptoriness, a priest in its blessings and anathemas, and, even though the eternal priesthood throughout the Church could cease to be, in it the sacerdotal principle would remain and would have a sway."

In earlier times "its supremacy was assailed by the arm of physical force," but "now the intellect is put in operation to sap the foundations of a power which the sword could not destroy." The threat is grandiloquently conveyed, but for all its fragile vulnerability, conscience has a strange, indestructible life:

> All through my day there has been a resolute warfare, I had almost said conspiracy against the rights of conscience, as I have described it. Literature and science have been embodied in great institutions in order to put it down. Noble buildings have been reared as fortresses against that spiritual, invisible influence which is too subtle for science and too profound for literature. Chairs in Universities have been made the seats of an antagonist tradition.

The secularized idea of conscience merely concerns "the right of thinking, speaking, writing, and acting" as one sees fit, "without any thought of God at all." Paradoxically, it has become "the very right and freedom of conscience to dispense with conscience." In effect, conscience "has been superseded by a counterfeit," namely, "the right of self-will."[58]

Were the pope himself to "speak against Conscience in the true sense of the word, he would commit a suicidal act. He would be cutting the ground from under his feet." Indeed, continues Newman, "we shall find that it is by the universal sense of right and wrong, the consciousness of transgression, the pangs of guilt, and the dread of retribution, as first principles deeply lodged in the hearts of men, it is thus and only thus, that he has gained his footing in the world and achieved his success." The "championship of the Moral Law and of conscience" is "his *raison d'être*," and the "fact of his mission is the answer to the complaints of those who feel the insufficiency of the natural light; and the insufficiency of that light is the justification of his mission." Once again Newman emphasizes the precarious nature of the moral sense, which "is at once the highest of all teachers, yet the least luminous; and the Church, the Pope, the Hierarchy are . . . the supply of an urgent demand." But if revelation is the fulfillment of natural religion, it is in no sense "independent of it":

"The Pope, who comes of Revelation, has no jurisdiction over Nature."[59]

Turning to the crucial question of the relation of individual conscience to authority, Newman begins by laying down the principle that since "conscience is not a judgment upon any speculative truth, any abstract doctrine, but bears immediately . . . on something to be done or not done," it "cannot come into direct collision with the Church's or the Pope's infallibility; which is engaged on general propositions, and in the condemnation of particular and given errors." Here Newman means by conscience not what moral theologians call *habitual* conscience, that is, conscience as it adheres to general moral norms and principles, but rather what they mean by *actual* conscience, that is, the judgment that this particular act here and now is to be done or not done as falling or not falling under the relevant moral precept. For example, my habitual conscience tells me that torturing children is wrong, but my actual conscience has to decide whether this particular punishment is or is not an act of torture. And so, Newman argues, because actual conscience is "a practical dictate," direct conflict is possible "only when the Pope legislates, or gives particular orders, and the like." However, "a Pope is not infallible in his laws, nor in his commands, nor in his acts of state, nor in his administration, nor in his public policy." After all, St. Peter was not infallible at Antioch when St. Paul disagreed with him, nor was Liberius when he excommunicated Athanasius.

However, the "dictate" of conscience, "in order to prevail against the voice of the Pope, must follow upon serious thought, prayer, and all available means of arriving at a right judgment on the matter in question." The onus of proof, then, lies on the individual conscience: "Unless a man is able to say to himself, as in the Presence of God, that he must not, and dare not, act upon the Papal injunction, he is bound to obey it, and would commit a great sin in disobeying it."[60] As usual, Newman's bold admission about the fallibility of the first pope in no way excludes a rigorous emphasis on loyalty and obedience to a legitimate superior. On the other hand, to obey a papal order which one seriously thinks is wrong would be a sin—even if one is culpably mistaken (a person may be to blame for having a false conscience, but not for acting in accordance with it). In the last analysis, conscience, however misguided, is supreme, and Newman concludes the discussion calmly, even casually, with the famous declaration:

> I add one remark. Certainly, if I am obliged to bring religion into after-dinner toasts, (which indeed does not seem quite the thing) I shall drink—to the Pope, if you please—still, to Conscience first, and to the Pope afterwards.[61]

Offices of the Church

Schematic, tidy blueprints are out of place in ecclesiology not only because the Church on earth is a living community made up of living people but also, as we have seen, because her "organization cannot be otherwise than complex, considering the many functions which she has to fulfil." Although the Church has always exercised its three main offices,

> they were developed in their full proportions one after another, in a succession of centuries; first, in the primitive time it was recognized as a worship, springing up and spreading in the lower ranks of society. . . . Then it seized upon the intellectual and cultivated class, and created a theology and schools of learning. Lastly it seated itself, as an ecclesiastical polity, among princes, and chose Rome for its centre.

The weight Newman places in the Preface to the *Via Media* on the theological office is significantly modified by important reservations: "Yet theology cannot always have its own way; it is too hard, too intellectual, too exact, to be always equitable, or to be always compassionate." Sometimes even a theologian in his writings has to "let his devout nature betray itself between the joints of his theological harness." Popular religion may, for example, reject a more accurate translation of the Bi-

ble because to "the devotional mind what is new and strange
is as repulsive, often as dangerous, as falsehood is to the scientific. Novelty is often error to those who are unprepared for
it, from the refraction with which it enters into their concep-
tions." However wrong the condemnation of Galileo,

> there was nothing wrong in censuring abrupt, startling, unsettling,
> unverified disclosures . . . at once uncalled for and inopportune,
> at a time when the limits of revealed truth had not as yet been
> ascertained. A man ought to be very sure of what he is saying,
> before he risks the chance of contradicting the word of God. It
> was safe, not dishonest, to be slow in accepting what nevertheless
> turned out to be true. Here is an instance in which the Church
> obliges Scripture expositors, at a given time or place, to be tender
> of the popular religious sense.

People's "imaginations" have to become accustomed to religious
changes, whereas "when science crosses and breaks the received
path of Revelation," religious people are criticized if "they show
hesitation to shift at a minute's warning their position, and to
accept as truths shadowy views at variance with what they have
ever been taught and have held." The modern idea holds that
it is "a great moral virtue to be fearless and thorough in inquiry
into facts," whereas the "pursuit of truth in the subject-matter
of religion . . . must always be accompanied by the fear of
error."[62] Elsewhere, Newman says: "What the genius of the
Church cannot bear is, changes in thought being hurried,
abrupt, violent—out of tenderness to souls, for unlearned and
narrow-minded men get unsettled and miserable. The great
thing is to move all together and then the change, as geological
changes, must be very slow."

In a letter, however, Newman emphasizes the role of theology
in preparing the Church for changes—"it is the arena on which
questions of development and change are argued out . . . it
prepares the way, accustoming the mind of Catholics to the
idea of the change." Because theology also, he explains, "protects" dogma by "forming a large body of doctrine which must
be got through before an attack can be made on the dogma,"

without theology "the dogma of the Church would be the raw flesh without skin—nay or a tree without leaves—for, as devotional feelings clothe the dogma on the one hand, so does the teaching of [theology] on the other."[63]

The Church allows much more freedom in devotion, which is "of a subjective and personal nature," than in doctrine. This contrast is accentuated if "ecclesiastical authority takes part with popular sentiment against a theological decision." A very early example would be the occasion at Antioch when St. Peter stopped associating with converts from paganism because of pressure from converts from Judaism, a lapse for which he was rebuked by St. Paul. However, Paul himself was ready to conform to Jewish customs when necessary, and the principle of "accommodation"—though it may be misapplied, as perhaps in the case of the Jesuit missionaries' adoption of Chinese customs—has always been practised by Christians since the earliest time.[64]

The theological office of the Church, then, may find itself in opposition to both the so-called political and pastoral offices. But equally, the political office may come into conflict with the other two offices. This office is, in fact, essential if the Church is to preserve its independence and freedom of action—as is illustrated by the Orthodox Church, "which has lost its political life, while its doctrine, and its ritual and devotional system, have little that can be excepted against." Like "a sovereign State," the Church has "to consolidate her several portions, to enlarge her territory, to keep up and to increase her various populations in this ever-dying, ever-nascent world, in which to be stationary is to lose ground, and to repose is to fail." So important is this aspect of the Church that a point of theology may at times actually be "determined on its expediency relatively to the Church's Catholicity," that is, "by the logic of facts, which at times overrides all positive laws and prerogatives, and reaches in its effective force to the very frontiers of immutable truths."[65] While not exaggerating this aspect of the Church, as was usual in the theology of his day, Newman refuses to ignore or downplay the institutional aspect of the Church.

This brilliantly seminal essay, the preface to the *Via Media*, concludes with the reflection that "whatever is great refuses to be reduced to human rule, and to be made consistent in its many aspects with itself." There should be no cause for surprise, then, if the Church "is an instance of the same law, presenting to us an admirable consistency and unity in word and deed, as her general characteristic, but crossed and discredited now and then by apparent anomalies."[66] That the Church, however, has a diversity of offices no more detracts from its essential oneness than the fact that it includes laity as well as hierarchy in its constitution. Newman's idea of the Church is of a wholeness and unity comprising a variety of elements and parts held together in creative tension, each sustained by mutual dependence rather than threatened by colliding interaction. It is also a vision comprehensive enough to see the Church both as a human institution and as a supernatural mystery.

6

SACRAMENTS

The Seven Sacraments

In the *Apologia* Newman mentions three sources for his deeply sacramental theology. First, in Joseph Butler's *Analogy of Religion* (1736) he read about the "idea of an analogy between the separate works of God," an idea which "leads to the conclusion that the system which is of less importance is economically or sacramentally connected with the more momentous system." Second, John Keble's *Christian Year* (1827) reinforced this idea of "what may be called, in a large sense of the word, the Sacramental system; that is, the doctrine that material phenomena are both the types and the instruments of real things unseen,—a doctrine, which embraces in its fulness, not only . . . Sacraments properly so called." Third, in the Alexandrian Fathers he found again "the mystical or sacramental principle," according to which "Holy Church in her sacraments . . . will remain, even to the end of the world, after all but a symbol of those heavenly facts which fill eternity."[1]

This profoundly sacramental vision meant that Newman never saw the formal sacraments of the Church as in any way isolated from a larger sacramental reality, and particularly from what modern Catholic theologians call the *primordial* sacrament, the Church herself. The seven Catholic sacraments, then, do not exhaust the sacramentality of Catholicism, but rather they

are the actions of the Church by which she principally constitutes and realizes her own sacramental character.

If the Church is the primordial sacrament, baptism is often
called by modern theologians the *primary* sacrament, since it
is the means to membership of the Church. This sacrament
was obviously of especial importance to the Anglican Newman
because it emphasizes the necessity of belonging to the Church
as opposed to the Evangelical stress on individual salvation
through faith. But for Newman, baptism was above all the
primary sacrament because through it the Christian receives
the gift of the Holy Spirit. In a sermon on a text from St. Paul's
first letter to the Corinthians ("By one Spirit are we all bap-
tized into one body"), Newman puts it like this:

> As there is One Holy Ghost, so there is one only visible Body of
> Christians . . . and one Baptism which admits men into it. This
> is implied in the text . . . But more than this is taught us in it;
> not only that the Holy Ghost is in the Church, and that Baptism
> admits into it, but that the Holy Ghost admits by means of Bap-
> tism, that the Holy Ghost baptizes; in other words, that each in-
> dividual member receives the gift of the Holy Ghost as a
> preliminary step, a condition, or means of his being incorporated
> into the Church; or, in our Saviour's words, that no one can enter,
> except he be regenerated in order to enter it.[2]

Thus baptism is crucial to our justification and salvation.

The sacraments, of course, are not magic, and Newman warns
his Anglican congregation in Oxford that "we but slowly enter
into the privileges of our baptism; we but gradually gain it."[3]
Certainly, it is obvious that "nothing shows, for some time, that
the Spirit of God is come into, and dwells in the child bap-
tized."[4] But Newman sees no reason to delay infant baptism:
"To defer Baptism till persons actually have repentance and
faith, is refusing to give medicine till a patient begins to get
well." There is another reason too:

> It is certain that children ought to be instructed in religious truth,
> as they can bear it, from the very first dawn of reason; clearly,

they are not to be left without a Christian training till they arrive at years of maturity. Now . . . Christ seems distinctly to connect teaching with Baptism, as if He intended to convey through it a blessing upon teaching, — "Go ye and teach all the nations, baptizing them." If children, then, are to be considered as under teaching, as learners in the school of Christ, surely they should be admitted into that school by Baptism.[5]

Modern western theologians, like their patristic forebearers and Orthodox theologians, group together as the three sacraments of initiation, baptism, confirmation, and eucharist. Similarly, in a letter written when he was an Anglican that clearly reflects the thought of the early Church, Newman writes:

Confirmation seals in their fulness, winds up and consigns, completes the entire round of those sanctifying gifts which are begun, which are given inchoately in Baptism. . . . it is properly an integral part of the Baptismal rite; I do not say of the essence, or an essential part, of Baptism, but an integral part, just as a hand is an integral part of our body, yet may be amputated without loss of life. And in ancient times it was administered at the time of Baptism, as its ratification.[6]

He regrets that it is not administered at an early age as in the Roman Catholic Church, "but we, having no rite of penance, seem to substitute this." As to the particular grace given in confirmation, it "is directed to arm the Christian against his . . . enemies, which, when entering into his field of trial, he at once meets." Newman hardly refers to confirmation in his Anglican sermons, but he does urge an early age for reception of the sacrament, with the implication that it is after all only the confirming of baptism: "When persons are young, before their minds are formed, ere they have sullied their baptismal robe, and contracted bad habits, this is the time for Confirmation, which conveys to them grace whereby they may perform that 'good work' which Baptism has begun in them."[7] Newman here seems much closer to the Eastern tradition that confirmation should closely follow baptism than to the idea that it is a sacrament which confirms a commitment taken at a mature age.

As we should expect, there are many more references to the eucharist in the Anglican sermons. Again, although it is not made explicit and it would have been quite contrary to Anglican practice at the time, the implication is surely that reception of holy communion should begin as soon as possible. In the East communion is given to babies; there seems no reason why this should not be so if we take Newman's words literally:

> Christ's blessed Supper is food to us altogether, *whatever* we are, soul, body, and all. . . . The forbidden fruit wrought in Adam unto death; but this is the fruit which makes us live for ever. Bread sustains us in this *temporal* life; the consecrated bread is the means of *eternal* strength for soul and body. Who could live this visible life without earthly food? And in the same general way the Supper of the Lord is the *"means"* of our living for ever. . . . We eat the sacred bread, and our bodies become sacred; they are not ours; they are Christ's; they are instinct with that flesh which saw not corruption; they are inhabited by His Spirit; they become immortal; they die but to appearance, and for a time; they spring up when their sleep is ended, and reign with Him for ever.[8]

Rejecting as an Anglican any attempt "to degrade the Eucharist from a Sacrament to a bare commemorative rite,"[9] Newman insists that what seems to the world "mere bread and wine" ("God has chosen the weak things of the world to confound the mighty")[10] is actually the body and blood of Christ — not in a literal carnal sense ("What was bread remains bread, and what was wine remains wine") but in a mysterious (as opposed to miraculous) way:

> He who is at the right hand of God, manifests Himself in that Holy Sacrament as really and fully as if He were visibly there. . . . Such is the glorious presence which faith sees in the Holy Communion, though every thing looks as usual to the natural man. Not gold or precious stones, pearls of great price or gold of Ophir, are to the eyes of faith so radiant as those lowly elements which

He, the Highest, is pleased to make the means of conveying to our hearts and bodies His own gracious self. Not the light of the sun sevenfold is so awfully bright and overpowering, if we could see as the Angels do, as that seed of eternal life, which by eating and drinking we lay up in our hearts against the day of His coming.[11]

As an Anglican preacher, Newman naturally did not speak of transubstantiation, but his theology of the real presence is deeply Catholic. In what he calls "the greatest and highest of all the Sacramental mysteries," Christ

is in it spiritually present, in the fulness of His death and of His resurrection. We call His presence in this Holy Sacrament a spiritual presence, not as if "spiritual" were but a name or mode of speech, and He were really absent, but by way of expressing that He who is present there can neither be seen nor heard; that He cannot be approached or ascertained by any of the senses; that he is not present in place, that He is not present carnally, though He is really present. And how this is, of course is a mystery.[12]

The words of institution at the Last Supper must signify "some very great mystery," otherwise "they must be a figurative way of declaring something which is not mysterious, but plain and intelligible. But is it conceivable that He who is the Truth and Love itself, should have used difficult words when plain words would do?" The actual "awful words," Newman argues, are "too clear and precise" to mean anything less than what they say. The "mystery of Christ's Presence in Holy Communion" may be incomprehensible, but so in a similar way is the miracle of the loaves with which it is closely connected in the gospel: "We know what is meant by saying that the blind saw, or the dead arose: but what is meant by saying that the loaves fed five thousand persons?"[13]

To the worshipper the truth of the real presence does not need demonstrating, Newman suggests in the powerful conclusion to a sermon called "Attendance on Holy Communion":

Nature fails, the sun shines not, and the moon is dim, the stars fall from heaven, and the foundations of the round world shake; but the Altar's light burns ever brighter; there are sights there which the many cannot see, and all above the tumults of earth the command is heard to show forth the Lord's death, and the promise that the Lord is coming

. . . Rest is better than toil; peace satisfies, and quietness disappoints not. These are sure goods. Such is the calm of the heavenly Jerusalem, which is the mother of us all; and such is their calm worship, the foretaste of heaven, who for a season shut themselves out from the world, and seek Him in invisible Presence, whom they shall see hereafter face to face.[14]

And to recall the spiritual experience is to confirm it:

We shall remember . . . how all things, light or darkness, sun or air, cold or freshness, breathed of Him,—of Him, the Lord of glory, who stood over us, and came down upon us, and gave Himself to us, and poured forth milk and honey for our sustenance, though we saw Him not. Surely we have all, and abound: we are full.

As a Catholic, what seems to have struck Newman more than anything else about the worship of the Catholic Church was devotion to the reserved sacrament. Shortly after he entered the Church he wrote enthusiastically to a friend, "It is such an incomprehensible blessing to have Christ in bodily presence in one's house, within one's walls, as swallows up all other privileges . . . To know that He is close by—to be able again and again through the day to go in to Him." So strongly did he feel this that he could say: "Now after tasting of the awful delight of worshipping God in His Temple, how unspeakably cold is the idea of a Temple without that Divine Presence! One is tempted to say what is the meaning, what is the use of it?" The sacrament reserved in the tabernacle was not simply a source of spiritual comfort, but it was what above all helped to produce "the deep impression of religion as an objective fact" which so impressed Newman as a convert to Catholicism.[16] And when he went to Italy to prepare for ordination to the Catholic priesthood, again and again he alluded to his overpowering sense of Christ sacramentally present in the churches—to that "Presence of our Undying Life, hidden but ever working," betokened by "the distant glimmering Lamp": "It is really most wonderful to see the Divine Presence looking out almost into the open streets from the various Churches. . . . I never knew what worship was, as an objective fact, till I entered the Catholic Church."[17] Nothing, he wrote, "has brought home to me so much the Unity of the Church, as the presence of its Divine Founder and Life wherever I go—All places are, as it were, one." It is not surprising that when the hero of his novel *Loss and Gain* attends a Catholic church for the first time, it is not the beauty of the liturgy that impresses him as much as "the Great Presence, which makes a Catholic Church different from every other place in the world."[18] The reservation of the consecrated eucharistic bread, then, has a special place for Newman among the various sacraments and sacramentals which ensure that "the Atonement of Christ is not a thing at a distance, or like the sun standing over against us and separated off from us, but that we are surrounded by an *atmosphere* and are in a medium, through which his warmth and light flow in upon us on every side."[19]

Priests are needed for the celebration of the sacraments, and there are a few references in the Anglican sermons to the awesome sacrament of holy orders. "Alas for us!" Newman groans, "we feel none of those terrors about it, which made the early Christians flee from it!" For them "it was so solemn a function, that the holier a man was, the less inclined he felt to undertake it."[20] For those who feel called to receive this sacrament, Newman has a solemn warning:

So again they who enter Holy Orders promise they know not what, engage themselves they know not how deeply, debar themselves of the world's ways they know not how intimately, find perchance they must cut off from them the right hand, sacrifice the desire of their eyes and the stirring of their hearts at the foot of the Cross, while they thought, in their simplicity, they were but choosing the easy life of quiet "plain men dwelling in tents."[21]

Newman did not preach as an Anglican about the sacrament of penance or reconciliation. The practice of private confession began to spread in the Church of England as a result of the Tractarian movement, and Newman himself heard his first confession in 1838; nevertheless, he preferred to avoid as far as possible theological controversy in his pastoral sermons. However, as he drew closer to Rome he came more and more to feel, as his private letters show, that without sacramental confession the pastoral work of a priest was pointless; indeed, he insisted on regular confession as a condition of membership of the quasi-monastic community he founded at Littlemore. As a Catholic, he wrote eloquently about the psychological value of confession:

> How many are the souls, in distress, anxiety or loneliness, whose one need is to find a being to whom they can pour out their feelings unheard by the world? Tell them out they must; they cannot tell them out to those whom they see every hour. They want to tell them and not to tell them; and they want to tell them out, yet be as if they be not told; they wish to tell them to one who is strong enough to bear them, yet not too strong to despise them; they wish to tell them to one who can at once advise and can sympathize with them; they wish to relieve themselves of a load, to gain a solace, to receive the assurance that there is one who thinks of them, and one to whom in thought they can recur, to whom they can betake themselves, if necessary, from time to time, while they are in the world. . . . If there is a heavenly idea in the Catholic Church, looking at it simply as an idea, surely, next after the Blessed Sacrament, Confession is such. . . . Oh what a soothing charm is there, which the world can neither give nor take away! Oh what piercing, heart-subduing tranquillity, provoking tears of joy, is poured, almost substantially and physically upon the soul . . . when the penitent at length rises, his God reconciled to him, his sins rolled away forever![22]

Sacraments and Sacramentality

Apart from discussions of particular points in his letters, Newman did not write about the sacraments as a Catholic, not even, curiously enough, in his published sermons. And so we must complete what must remain an incomplete account with a few observations on the sacraments in general, again mostly culled from the Anglican sermons. As a reminder that Newman had a larger sacramental vision than was common among Catholic theologians of the time, for whom sacramentality tended to mean exclusively the seven sacraments, there is a remarkable passage in one of the sermons where he says that the Christian "will see Christ revealed to his soul amid the ordinary actions of the day, as by a sort of sacrament."[23] He remarks elsewhere on the essential ordinariness of the sacraments: in contrast to "the Jewish ordinances" which were "long and laborious, expensive or irksome," the Christian sacraments "are so simple, so brief, with so little of outward substance, that the mind is not detained for a moment from Him who works by means of them, but takes them for what they really are, only so far outward as to serve for a medium of the heavenly gift." As the actions of the Church, they are also the actions of Christ, who "shines through them, as through transparent bodies, without impediment."[24] In the Church's sacraments, Newman declares in a magnificently mysterious passage,

is manifested in greater or less degree, according to the measure of each, that Incarnate Saviour, who is one day to be our Judge, and who is enabling us to bear His presence then, by imparting it to us in measure now. A thick black veil is spread between this world and the next. We mortal men range up and down it, to and fro, and see nothing. There is no access through it into the next world. In the Gospel this veil is not removed; it remains, but every now and then marvellous disclosures are made to us of what is behind it. At times we seem to catch a glimpse of a Form which we shall hereafter see face to face. We approach, and in spite of the darkness, our hands, or our head, or our brow, or our lips become, as it were, sensible of the contact of something more than earthly. We know not where we are, but we have been bathing in water, and a voice tells us that it is blood. Or we have a mark signed upon our foreheads, and it spake of Calvary. Or we recollect a hand laid upon our heads, and surely it had the print of nails in it, and resembled His who with a touch gave sight to the blind and raised the dead. Or we have been eating and drinking; and it was not a dream surely, that One fed us from His wounded side, and renewed our nature by the heavenly meat He gave.[25]

As "the embodied forms of the Spirit of Christ,"[26] the sacraments "persuade" by their "tenderness and mysteriousness." Indeed, says Newman, it was "the rule of the Primitive Church" to teach "the more Sacred Truths ordinarily by rites and ceremonies," for it was far more "reverential" that doctrine should be taught through sacraments rather than sermons, so that, for example, the eucharist is "the continual revelation of the Incarnation."[27]

The great doctrine of the indwelling of the Holy Spirit, and so of the Trinity, is, as we have seen, the most important theological rediscovery that Newman himself made from his study of the New Testament and the Fathers. In the *Lectures on Justification* Newman connects the theory of justification by faith alone with the neglect of the sacramental dimension of Christianity: whenever "the Living Presence conveyed in the Sacraments" is forgotten, "an opening has been at once made for the meagre and artificial doctrine of a nominal righteousness," since there are so many passages in Scripture "which speak of the Atonement as still living in Christians, that if we will not enforce them literally, we must be content to hear them explained away into a mere imputation of it in God's dealings with us, or into a contemplation of it by our faith." In fact, argues Newman, faith, "considered as an instrument" of our justification "is always secondary to the Sacraments." St. Paul himself, although he had seen Christ and believed, had to have his sins washed away in baptism. The

New Testament never speaks of faith washing away sins or initiating or beginning the Christian life: "The silence of Scripture on this point is the more remarkable from the circumstance that so many high gifts—sanctification, eternal life, and resurrection of the body—*are* connected in Scripture with faith; all but the new birth; all but the first step, and this is . . . said to be through Baptism." To the objection that in fact faith precedes baptism, Newman replies:

> Though faith comes before Baptism, yet before Baptism it is not the instrument of justification, but only one out of a number of qualifications necessary for being justified. Nothing is said in Scripture of faith before Baptism, that is not said of repentance, or of the resolve to lead a new life, which also are necessary conditions, together with faith, in order to Baptism."

Newman concludes that faith

> justifies only, in two ways, as the only inward *instrument*, and as the only *symbol*. Viewed as an instrument, it unites the soul to Christ through the Sacraments; viewed as a symbol it shows forth the doctrine of free grace. Hence it is the instrument of justification after Baptism; it is a symbol both before and after.

A pithy sentence sums up his view of the matter: "Justification comes *through* the Sacraments; it is received *by* faith; *consists* in God's inward presence; and *lives* in obedience." Or, in other words, "whether we say we are justified by faith, or by works or by Sacraments, all these but mean this one doctrine, that we are justified by grace, which is given through Sacraments, impetrated by faith, manifested in works."[28]

In the *Lectures on Justification* Newman also argues that religion implies "the belief in such sensible tokens of God's favour, as the Sacraments are accounted by the Church," for religion "is of a personal nature, and implies the acknowledgement of a particular Providence, of a God speaking, not merely to the world at large, but to this person or that, to one and not to another." The Bible "is a common possession, and speaks to one man as much and as little as to his neighbour," but human

nature "requires something special," something of a highly personal character.[29] And so it is that Christ comes to each of
us individually and personally through the sacraments:

> Our Lord, by becoming man, has found a way whereby to sanctify
> that nature, of which His own manhood is the pattern specimen.
> He inhabits us personally, and this inhabitation is effected by the
> channel of the Sacraments.

Through "this indwelling," Christ is the "immediate" source of
"spiritual life to each of His elect individually." For "He mingles
Himself with the faithful individually, through the mysteries."
Thus "while we are in the flesh, soul and body become, by the
indwelling of the Word, so elevated above their natural state,
so sacred, that to profane them is a sacrilege."[30] This sacramental
divinization of human nature through the indwelling of Christ
personally in the believer bears no resemblance to that abstract
and impersonal theology of sacramental grace so criticized by
modern Catholic theologians as unscriptural.

7

CHRISTIAN LIFE

Holiness

If one had to say what is the dominant theme of the eight volumes of *Parochial and Plain Sermons*, which contain the bulk of Newman's published pastoral sermons, the answer would surely be: the call to holiness. The idea that the whole Church, the whole people of God, are called to be holy was not in Newman's day the truism that it is now in the Catholic Church; until the Second Vatican Council there was a widespread feeling that holiness was a condition that pertained principally to priests and religious. Certainly, as an Anglican preacher, Newman entertained no such restricted view.

The very first sermon of the first volume of *Parochial and Plain Sermons* is entitled "Holiness Necessary for Future Blessedness." In it Newman exhorts his congregation, "Be you content with nothing short of perfection." But the first thing we notice about this call is that there is nothing vaguely uplifting about it. It is not an invitation to entertain spiritual feelings or thoughts of holiness. There is nothing sentimental about Newman's spirituality: "Is not holiness the result of many patient, repeated efforts after obedience, gradually working on us, and first modifying and then changing our hearts?"[1] The challenge may be a hard one, but Newman assures, or rather warns, us that we have no excuse for failing to meet it if we are Christians:

119

We dwell in the full light of the Gospel, and the full grace of the Sacraments. We ought to have the holiness of Apostles. There is no reason except our own wilful corruption, that we are not by this time walking in the steps of St. Paul or St. John, and following them as they followed Christ.[2]

Newman is a preacher not of glowing words but of harsh realities—realities that arise out of the obligation imposed by baptism to lead the Christian life to the full:

To love our brethren with a resolution which no obstacles can overcome, so as almost to consent to an anathema on ourselves, if so be we may save those who hate us,—to labour in God's cause against hope, and in the midst of sufferings,—to read the events of life, as they occur, by the interpretation which Scripture gives them, and that, not as if the language were strange to us, but to do it promptly,—to perform all our relative daily duties most watchfully,—to check every evil thought, and bring the whole mind into captivity to the law of Christ,—to be patient, cheerful, forgiving, meek, honest, and true,—to persevere in this good work till death, making fresh and fresh advances towards perfection—and after all, even to the end, to confess ourselves unprofitable servants, nay, to feel ourselves corrupt and sinful creatures, who (with all our proficiency) would still be lost unless God bestowed on us His mercy in Christ;—these are some of the difficult realities of religious obedience, which we must pursue, and which the Apostles in high measure attained, and which we may well bless God's holy name, if He enables us to make our own.[3]

The trouble with most people is not that they do not "act up to their standard, but it is their standard that is low."[4] And their standard is low because they do not want to be holy. With characteristic psychological realism Newman puts his finger on the central reason why Christians are not better than they are: they do not want to be. In one of the sermons he exhorts his hearers not to strive for holiness but to strive for the desire for holiness; in doing so he sets out a remarkably comprehensive, practical program for a spiritual life in a marvelous passage that ends on a note of lyrical beauty:

> Let us strive and pray that the love of holiness may be created within our hearts; and then acts will follow, such as befit us and our circumstances, in due time, without our distressing ourselves to find what they should be. You need not attempt to draw any precise line between what is sinful and what is only allowable: look up to Christ, and deny yourselves every thing, whatever its character, which you think He would have you relinquish. You need not calculate and measure, if you love much: you need not perplex yourselves with points of curiosity, if you have a heart to venture after Him. True, difficulties will sometimes arise, but they will be seldom. He bids you take up your cross; therefore accept the daily opportunities which occur of yielding to others, when you need not yield, and of doing unpleasant services, which you might avoid. He bids those who would be highest, live as the lowest: therefore, turn from ambitious thoughts, and (as far as you religiously may) make resolves against taking on you authority and rule. He bids you sell and give alms; therefore, hate to spend money on yourself. Shut your ears to praise, when it grows loud: set your face like a flint, when the world ridicules, and smile at its threats. Learn to master your heart, when it would burst forth into vehemence, or prolong a barren sorrow, or dissolve into unseasonable tenderness. Curb your tongue, and turn away your eye, lest you fall into temptation. Avoid the dangerous air which relaxes you, and brace yourself upon the heights. Be up at prayer "a great while before day," and seek the true, your only Bridegroom, "by night on your bed." So shall self-denial become natural to you, and a change come over you, gently and imperceptibly; and, like Jacob, you will lie down in the waste, and will soon see Angels, and a way opened for you into heaven.[5]

The contrast in tone between that final gliding sentence in which holiness is effortlessly achieved and the abrupt, peremptory catalogue of the demands of self-denial is very characteristic of Newman's style of preaching. The sermons are as merciless and unrelenting in their insistence on the highest ideals of Christian life as they are soothing and caressing in their celebration of the happiness of holiness. And the rhythm of the prose alternates correspondingly between the staccato and mellifluous:

> . . . the world is your enemy, and the flesh is your enemy. Come to God, and beg of Him grace to devote yourself to Him. Beg of Him the will to follow Him; beg of Him the power to obey Him. O how comfortable, pleasant, sweet, soothing, and satisfying is it to lead a holy life,—the life of Angels! It is difficult at first: but with God's grace, all things are possible. O how pleasant to have done with sin! how good and joyful to flee temptation and to resist evil! how meet, and worthy, and fitting, and right, to die unto sin, and to live unto righteousness![6]

It is rare for a preacher to emphasize so evenhandedly both the difficulties and the blessings of a Christian life.

The call to holiness rings out uncompromisingly through the sermons: "Let us not be content with ourselves; let us not make our own hearts our home, or this world our home, or our friends our home; let us look out for a better country, that is, a heavenly." But the summons is not merely admonitory or rhetorical, for the purpose behind the message is as serious as the reward is real:

> Blessed are they who give the flower of their days, and their strength of soul and body to Him; blessed are they who in their youth turn to Him who gave His life for them, and would fain give it to them and implant it in them, that they may live for ever. Blessed are they who resolve—come good, come evil, come sunshine, come tempest, come honour, come dishonour—that He shall be their Lord and Master, their King and God![7]

Nor is there anything unreal about the means to the end that Newman so insistently impresses on his hearers. Indeed, the very practicality often contains a surprise. Thus, we should expect Newman to urge the necessity of prayer, but the actual content of the prayer he recommends is not, perhaps, what we might anticipate: he does not advise his hearers to pray for holiness so much as to "pray for His saving help to change their likings and dislikings, their tastes, their views, their wills, their hearts."[8] For obviously there is little point in praying to be holy if one does not particularly want to be holy and if it is the wish to be holy for which one should in fact be praying.

Again, we might assume from the impassioned language of the preacher and his refusal to be content with anything but the realization of the highest ideals that the means to the end would be correspondingly momentous. But in fact what is so striking about Newman's spirituality is its ordinariness and unpretentiousness. He warns, for example, that "to take up the cross of Christ is no great action done once for all," but "it consists in the continual practice of small duties which are distasteful to us"; for "the self-denial which is pleasing to Christ consists in little things." A great deal hangs on small acts of apparently little consequence. Thus one "apparently small defect will influence your whole spirit and judgment in all things," since "your judgment of persons, and of events, and of actions, and of doctrines, and your spirit towards God and man, your faith in the high truths of the Gospel, and your knowledge of your duty, all depend in a strange way on this strict endeavour to observe the whole law, on this self-denial in those little things in which obedience is a self-denial." This emphasis on "daily self-denial"[9] (as opposed to great, occasional self-denials) being the key to true Christian belief and practice is very much in line with Newman's insistence on the connection between moral and intellectual integrity. It is also a great witness to Christianity: "how great a profession, and yet a profession how unconscious and modest, arises from the mere ordinary manner in which any strict Christian lives."[10]

Newman draws our attention to two important psychological truths. First is the aspect of habituation: "there is the most close and remarkable connexion between small observances and the permanence of our chief habits and practices." Second is the peculiar mortification involved in regular discipline: "Nothing is more difficult than to be disciplined and regular in our religion. It is very easy to be religious by fits and starts, and to keep up our feelings by artificial stimulants; but regularity seems to trammel us, and we become impatient."[11] Again, too, it is worth noting "how mysteriously little things are in this world connected with great; how single moments, improved or wasted, are the salvation or ruin of all-important interests."[12] And so "That little deed, suddenly exacted of us, almost suddenly resolved on and executed, may be as though a gate into the second or third heaven."[13] Of this kind of hidden, obscure holiness, in which "the silent duties of every day . . . are blest to the sufficient sanctification of thousands, whom the world knows not of," Mary is herself "a memorial."[14]

As a Catholic, Newman was to observe: "I have ever made consistency the mark of a Saint."[15] Already in his Anglican sermons he insists again and again on consistency as the note of authentic Christian faith:

> General conscientiousness is the only assurance we can have of possessing it; and at this we must aim, determining to obey God consistently, with a jealous carefulness about all things, little and great. . . . As far then as a man has reason to hope that he is *consistent*, so far may he humbly trust that he has true faith.[16]

If we reach heaven through small acts, the opposite is also true for Newman: "men do not lose their souls by some one extraordinary act, but by a course of acts."[17] In fact, however, the real test lies only in a limited range of actions: "Now let every one consider what his weak point is; in that is his test. His trial is not in those things which are easy to him, but in that one thing, in those several things, whatever they are, in which to do his duty is against his nature."[18] The nature of a person is formed by his or her habits, and Newman warns severely: "Any *one* deliberate habit of sin incapacitates a man for receiving the gifts of the Gospel."[19] Moreover, "sinful habits . . . clog" the "exercise" of a person's will.[20] Because "no habit is formed at once . . . the flame of religion in the heart" needs to be "purified and strengthened by long practice and experience."[21] By "*systematically*" trying to be good, we become good.[22]

Holiness is rare simply because it "is hard, indeed, to find a man who gives himself up honestly to his Saviour."[23] There is "nothing so rare as strict obedience, unreserved submission to God's will, uniform conscientiousness in doing [one's] duty."[24] Most Christians "wish to be saved, but in their own way; they wish (as it were) to capitulate upon terms, to carry off their goods with them." It is usual to have "a reserve" in one's "obedience," to keep a "corner" in one's "heart" to oneself; and "a half purpose" is as different from "a whole one" as "ice from the flowing stream."[25] The secret of holiness is rather to depend on Christ: "All of us must rely on something; all must look up to, admire, court, make themselves one with something. Most men cast in their lot with the visible world." Hence holy people seem to the world "like *foreigners*."[26] And the "holier a man is, the less he is understood by men of the world."[27]

Newman agrees with St. Paul that love "is the root of all holy dispositions, and grows and blossoms into them"; it is "the material (so to speak) out of which all graces are made, the quality of mind which is the fruit of regeneration, and in which the Spirit dwells." For "we love for no cause beyond itself: we love, because it is our nature to love; and it is our nature, because God the Holy Ghost has made it our nature." And so love "is the seed of holiness, and grows into all excellences, not indeed destroying their peculiarities, but making them what they are." It is "the first element" of holiness, as faith is of religion. It is "the motion within us of the new spirit, the holy and renewed heart which God the Holy Ghost gives us." Faith can make "a hero," but "love makes a saint."[28]

As "habits of holiness are matured, principle, reason, and self-discipline are unnecessary; a moral instinct takes their place in the breast, or rather, to speak more reverently, the Spirit is sovereign there. There is no calculation, no struggle, no self-regard, no investigation of motives. We act from love."[29] True holiness has an effortlessness about it once it has been attained, as Newman conveys in a beautiful and moving passage:

Then we do everything thankfully and joyfully, when we are temples of Christ, with His Image set up in us. Then it is that we mix with the world without loving it, for our affections are given to another. We can bear to look on the world's beauty, for we have no heart for it. We are not disturbed at its frowns, for we live not in its smiles. We rejoice in the House of Prayer, because He is there "whom our soul loveth." We can condescend to the poor and lowly, for they are the presence of Him who is Invisible. We are patient in bereavement, adversity, or pain, for they are Christ's tokens.

Certainly, without holiness we are not fit for heaven, since the "only qualification which will avail us for heaven is the love of God." It is not enough to "keep from gross sinning," since love alone "changes our whole being" and "makes us live."[30]

There are many accounts and descriptions of holiness in the Anglican sermons. To discover "its secret pleasure" one has to commit one's life totally to Christ, as otherwise one will be "dead to the most lively and wonderful of all pleasures." Newman does not hesitate to appeal passionately to his hearers' self-interest:

Nothing is so pleasant as God's service to those *to whom* it is plea-sant. The pleasures of sin are not to be compared in fulness and intensity to the pleasures of holy living. The pleasures of holiness are far more pleasant to the holy, than the pleasures of sin to the sinner. O that I could get you to believe this! O that you had a heart to feel it and know it! O that you had a heart to taste God's pleasures and to make proof of them; to taste and see how gracious the Lord is![31]

It is not just holiness that Newman recommends but "the *beauty* of holiness,"

which consists in tender and eager affection towards one Lord and Saviour: which is, in the case of the Christian, what beauty of person is to the outward man, so that through God's mercy our souls may have, not strength and health only, but a sort of bloom and comeliness; and that as we grow older in body, we may, year by year, grow more youthful in spirit.[32]

But we cannot "begin to discern the beauty of holiness" until we "labour to change our nature, through God's help, and to serve Him truly."[33] This involves rejecting the world: "He who has thrown himself out of this world, alone can overcome it; he who has cut himself loose of it, alone cannot be touched by it; he alone can be courageous, who does not fear it; he alone firm, who is not moved by it; he alone severe with it, who does not love it." As a result, "the world scorns and ridicules even more than it hates" the holy person, "a character which seems to court insult, because it endures it," as "unfit for life," "tame and spiritless," "a dreamer"—and yet, Newman points out, "such is the character of which Christ gave us the pattern; such was the character of Apostles; such the character which has ever conquered the world."[34] Growth in holiness brings its own self-contempt, for "the more your soul becomes one with Him who deigns to dwell within it, the more it sees with His eyes."[35] Still, "the souls of holy men . . . have a well of peace springing up within them unfathomable . . . a deep, silent, hidden peace, which the world sees not,—like some well in a retired and shady place, difficult of access." The "true life" of the holy person is what "he is when left to himself and to his God": "He can bear himself; he can (as it were) joy in himself, for it is the grace of God within him, it is the presence of the Eternal Comforter, in which he joys."[36]

The real source of Christian holiness, then, is ultimately the "indwelling of the Holy Spirit," for "Christ brings us into it by coming to us through His Spirit; and, as His Spirit is holy, we are holy, if we are in the state of grace. Christ is present in that heart which He visits with His grace."[37] We Christians, therefore,

have a spiritual principle in us, if we did but exert it, so great, so wondrous, that all the powers in the visible world, all the conceivable forces and appetites of matter, all the physical miracles which are at this day in process of discovery, almost superseding time and space, dispensing with numbers, and rivalling mind, all these powers of nature are nothing to this gift within us."[38]

There might well seem to be no excuse for not being holy, but in fact the holy are always "the few, and the unholy the many," for through the ages "out of the whole number of persons blessed with the means of grace, few only have duly availed them of this great benefit."[39]

The truth is that in spite of grace, our human cooperation is required. And in spite of his mystical theology of the indwelling of the Holy Spirit, Newman is very anxious in his preaching to stress not so much the role of the Spirit as the very practical part that we must play through exercising the gift of free will. It is this emphasis on human responsibility as opposed to divine initiative that very largely explains why his Anglican sermons seem so severe. The ultimate fount of holiness is indeed the indwelling Spirit, but holiness is, "as it were, wrought out of sin, the result of a continual struggle,—not spontaneous nature, but habitual self-command." Holiness has to be attained "through infirmity, because man's very condition is a fallen one, and in passing out of the country of sin, he necessarily passes through it."[40] Newman hardly underestimates the difficulty of even the smallest victories over sin, suggesting that we may congratulate ourselves "if, for all our infirmities, we can point to some occasions on which we have sacrificed anything for God's service, or to any habit of sin or evil tendency of nature which we have more or less overcome, or to any habitual self-denial which we practise, or to any work which we have accomplished to God's honour and glory."[41] We have grace, but "what we want is the will; and it is our own fault that we have it not." It is "a very practical plain matter" that "what we lack is the real, simple, earnest, sincere inclination and aim to use what God has given us, and what we have in us." Have we ever actually "*willed*" to rid ourselves of a bad habit? To be sure, "by nature we cannot will, but by grace we can": God gives us the power, but we have to use the power he gives. And by "beginning by little and little," we go on to "*will* great things."[42]

The Means to Holiness

If holiness is the end of the Christian life, what are the means we must use to attain to it?

The first step in any kind of spirituality must be conversion. But conversion need not mean only a dramatic event; as always, Newman is more interested in gradual but steady development and growth. He was particularly suspicious of the sudden emotional conversions favored by the kind of Evangelical Christians "who deny the grace of baptism, and think that a man is converted to God all at once."[43] A true conversion cannot take place all at one time:

> When men change their religious opinions really and truly, it is not merely their opinions that they change, but their hearts; and this evidently is not done in a moment—it is a slow work; nevertheless, though gradual, the change is often not uniform, but proceeds . . . by fits and starts, being influenced by external events, and other circumstances.

It may often seem "as if the very time of conversion . . . were sudden," but in reality there may be no "suddenness in the matter" at all—but, rather,

> at length the inward growth forces itself forward, forces on the opinions accompanying it, and the dead outward surface of error, which has no root . . . from some accidental occurrence, suddenly falls off; suddenly,—just as a building might suddenly fall, which had been going many years, and which falls at this moment rather than that, in consequence of some chance cause . . . which we cannot detect.

Even St. Paul's character was not changed at his dramatic conversion, "but merely directed to other and higher objects, and purified; it was his creed that was changed, and his soul by regeneration." Some sudden conversions are obviously not genuine because they do not last, but there are other sudden conversions which do last and yet are "not from God," as is shown by their "moroseness, inhumanity, and unfitness for this world":

"Men who change through strong passion and anguish become as hard and as rigid as stone or iron." And Newman traces back such grim religious conversions to "some form of selfishness and pride."[44] Conversion has to go on throughout the Christian life until the "perfect Christian state" is reached, "in which our duty and our pleasure are the same, when what is right and true is natural to us."[45] As we should expect from his account of faith, Newman is emphatic that the real barrier to continuing conversion is a moral one, for "a previous immoral life is . . . a grievous permanent hindrance and a curse to a man, after he has turned to God."[46]

Conversion involves repentance, and like conversion, repentance has to continue throughout the Christian life.

> Repentance is a work carried on at diverse times, and but gradually and with many reverses perfected. . . . we are *ever* but beginning; the most perfect Christian is to himself but a beginner, a penitent prodigal, who has squandered God's gifts, and comes to Him to be tried over again, not as a son, but as a hired servant.[47]

Because we sin constantly, we have to repent constantly, for "sin neglected not only stains and infects the soul, but it becomes habitual. It perverts and deforms the soul; it permanently enfeebles, cripples, or mutilates us. Let us then rid ourselves of it at once day by day, as of dust on our hands and faces." This harping on the need to repent may jar on contemporary Christian ears, but it comes from a great master of the spiritual life who not only never loses sight of the ideal of holiness but who is also an acute student of psychology. "You cannot repent too much," Newman declares in a robustly and characteristically colloquial tone:

> Come to God day by day, intreating Him for all the sins of your whole life up to the very hour present. This is the way to keep your baptismal robe bright. Let it be washed as your garments of this world are, again and again; washed in the most holy, most precious, most awfully salutary of all streams, His blood, who is without blemish and without spot.[48]

Although there is "no principle of *growth*" without regular repentance, even repentance does not remove the "present consequences" of "past offences, whether outward or inward," since "sin *leaves* a burden upon the soul, which has to be got rid of." As we shall see, the Anglican Newman sees the need for purgatory, as he indicates when he wonders whether "a debt is not standing against [Christians] for their past sins, and is not now operating or to operate to their disadvantage. What its payment consists in, and how it will be exacted, is quite another question, and a hidden one." Newman even suggests that "a long repentance may be the only remedy for . . . past deeds" to ensure that the repentance is sincere and the sins "absolutely forgiven."[50] And this raises the question, "What is repentance? is repentance the work of a day? is it a mere word? is it enough to say, 'I am sorry?' . . . What degree or kind of feeling is enough? Considering how our hearts deceive us, is even the most passionate feeling to be trusted?" But even so we must "persevere in prayer for pardon through our lives," for Scripture tells us that we do not gain pardon by "once asking" but by persistent prayer. This may seem to imply a permanent "state of mingled hope and fear, of peace and anxiety, of grace and of insecurity," but then "such a waiting and persevering temper" is intended to be the mark of a Christian.[51]

The point is that we have to grow into repentance: "The truest kind of repentance as little comes at first, as perfect conformity to any other part of God's Law. It is gained by long practice—it will come at length."[52] Not that repentance is desirable for its own sake: one should not "suppose that repentance makes all straight and even, and puts a man in the same place as if he had never departed from grace given."[53] Again, Newman warns, "Many as are the passages in the New Testament, which describe a state of salvation, none of them, excepting one or two, mention pardon as among the *continual* privileges of that state, or otherwise than as a gift once given on entering into it." There the "one broad idea of a state of salvation is one, not of sinning and being forgiven, but of holiness"; the New Testament assumes Christians to be "in a higher state, and gives little information how to treat them as we actually find them." Newman severely criticizes the Evangelical idea that "faith is all in all" and that "the only business of a Christian is, not to be holy, but to have faith." On this view "a state of salvation" is "nothing more or less than a state *in which* our sins are forgiven; a state of mere acceptance, not of substantial holiness": but in fact the New Testament shows that "it is a state in which there are not sins of every kind to forgive; and that, if a man commits them, so far from being forgiven *by* his state, he falls at once *from* his state by committing them."[54]

The psychological insight of the preacher is such that he can hardly be accused of underestimating the difficulty of conversion and repentance. Without grace, both are impossible: "God alone can change us; God alone can give us the desires, affections, principles, views, and tastes which a change implies." Humanly speaking, the difficulty is daunting:

> We do not like to be new-made; we are afraid of it; it is throwing us out of all our natural ways, of all that is familiar to us. We feel as if we should not *be* ourselves any longer, if we do not keep some portion of what we have been hitherto; and much as we prefer in general terms to wish to be changed, when it comes to the point, when particular instances of change are presented to us, we shrink from them, and are content to remain unchanged.

Newman's discomforting realism cuts through the usual bland pieties and shows very specifically why the Bible tells us we need new hearts and why the radical change implied by conversion is so hard: "You cannot bear to be other than you are. Life would seem a blank to you, were you other."[55]

After so severe an exposition of repentance, discovering that it must have a bright as well as a bleak side to it may come as something of a relief:

> Gloom is no Christian temper; that repentance is not real, which has not love in it; that self-chastisement is not acceptable, which is not sweetened by faith and cheerfulness. We must live in sunshine, even when we sorrow; we must live in God's presence, we

must not shut ourselves up in our own hearts, even when we are reckoning up our past sins.

This is proved through a consideration of its essential ingredient: "true repentance cannot be without the thought of God; it has the thought of God, for it seeks Him; and it seeks Him, because it is quickened with love; and even sorrow must have a sweetness, if love be in it."[56]

The emphasis on both the cheerful and the gloomy aspects of repentance is only a part of Newman's general spirituality, which in turn reflects his theological concern for keeping a balance between the cross and the resurrection. Thus he stresses in his preaching that "we must fear and be in sorrow, before we can rejoice. The Gospel must be a burden before it comforts and brings us peace."[57] Without severity, love itself will no longer be true love: "I wish I saw any prospect of this element of zeal and holy sternness springing up among us, to temper and give character to the languid, unmeaning benevolence which we misname Christian love." To speak only of God's love and never of his wrath is spiritually debilitating. Instead, Newman urges, it is necessary to "condense" one's "feelings by a severe discipline" and to be "loving in the midst of firmness, strictness, and holiness."[58] The problem is that people "find a difficulty in conceiving how Christians can have hope without certainty, sorrow and pain without gloom, suspense with calmness and confidence; how they can believe that in one sense they are in the light of God's countenance, and that in another sense they have forfeited it."[59] Given the fallen state of human nature, Newman has no doubt that what tends to be the neglected side of Christianity needs the most emphasis: those "who seem only to fear, or to have very little joy in religion . . . are in a more hopeful state than those who only joy and do not fear at all"—although, admittedly, the latter "are not altogether in a right state."[60] Ideally, faith is "always sorrowing" with Christ in his death, "while it rejoices" in his resurrection.[61] This is why "none rejoice in Easter-tide less than those who have not grieved in Lent." Similarly, it is our own "previous humiliation" which "sobers our joy" and "alone secures it to us."[62] Again, it is the "duty of fearing" that "does but perfect our joy; that joy alone is true Christian joy, which is informed and quickened by fear, and made thereby sober and reverent." The "paradox" of combining two such contradictory emotions is "fulfilled in the case of men of advanced holiness," which is why they are "accused of the most opposite faults."[63] Such a union of feelings arises out of the mystery of the redemption:

> Christ's going to the Father is at once a source of sorrow, because it involves His absence; and of joy, because it involves His presence. And out of the doctrine of His resurrection and ascension, spring those Christian paradoxes, often spoken of in Scripture, that we are sorrowing, yet always rejoicing; as having nothing, yet possessing all things.[64]

According to Newman, the "world" always "chooses some one or other peculiarity of the Gospel as the badge of its particular fashion for the time being." The contemporary age has a special concern for social justice: "There is a steady regard for the rights of individuals . . . for the interest of the poorer classes." But what the present time lacks, Newman thinks, is what he calls "firmness, manliness, godly severity." The problem for the Christian in every age is "the reconciling in our conduct opposite virtues," whereas it is comparatively easy "to cultivate single virtues" like compassion.[65]

We have already touched on some instances of the severer side of the gospel which Newman regards as the neglected means to holiness. Thus no amount of religious feeling and talk can take "the place of careful obedience, of that *self-denial* which is the very substance of true practical religion."[66] "The evidence of *self-denial*" is our assurance that we are "true servants" of God.[67] The fact that Christ led "so mortified" a life on earth shows that "austerity" is "man's glory."[68] And the Christian "will be touched by the thought of His cross far more by bearing it after Him, than by glowing accounts of it."[69] There is an analogy between our physical and our spiritual life: "As health and exercise and regular diet are necessary to strength of the body, so an enfeebling and afflicting of the natural man, a chastising and afflicting of soul and body, are necessary to the exaltation of the soul."[70] Newman's psychological realism also indicates that religion without self-denial is impossible:

> Self-denial of some kind or other is involved . . . in the very notion of renewal and holy obedience. To change our hearts is to learn to love things which we do not naturally love—to unlearn the love of this world; but this involves, of course, a thwarting of our natural wishes and tastes. To be righteous and obedient implies self-command; but to possess power we must have gained it; nor can we gain it without a vigorous struggle, a persevering warfare against ourselves. The very notion of being religious implies self-denial, because by nature we do not love religion.

The Christian is called to self-denial even "in things lawful because he is aware of his own weakness and liability to sin; he dares not walk on the edge of a precipice; instead of going to the extreme of what is allowable, he keeps at a distance from evil, that he may be safe." So, for example, anger "is not in itself a sinful feeling; but in man, constituted as he is, it is so highly dangerous to indulge it, that self-denial here is a duty from mere prudence." The opposite of self-denial leads inevitably to the worship of idols:

> Nothing is so likely to corrupt our hearts, and to seduce us from God, as to surround ourselves with comforts,—to have things our own way,—to be the centre of a sort of world, whether of things animate or inanimate, which minister to us. For then, in turn, we shall depend on them; they will become necessary to us; their very service and adulation will lead us to trust ourselves to them, and to idolize them.[71]

"Daily self-denials" help us to avoid sin: deliberately looking for them "proves your earnestness, and because by doing so you strengthen your general power of self-mastery, and come to have such an habitual command of yourself, as will be a defence ready prepared when the season of temptation comes." To prove you are serious about your Christian faith, "Make some sacrifice,

do some distasteful thing, which you are not actually obliged
to do . . . to bring home to your mind that in fact you do
love your Saviour." Nor is Newman vague on the practicalities
of the self-renunciation he envisages: "Let your very rising from
your bed be a self-denial; let your meals be self-denials. Determine to yield to others in things indifferent, to go out of your
way in small matters, to inconvenience yourself . . . rather
than you should not meet with your daily discipline." And he
provides a startling image to prove his point:

> In dreams we sometimes move our arms to see if we are awake
> or not, and so we are awakened. This is the way to keep your heart
> awake also. Try yourself daily in little deeds, to prove that your
> faith is more than a deceit.[72]

For our love of Christ is shown normally "not in great matters,
not in giving up house and lands for His sake, but in making
little sacrifices which the world would ridicule, if it knew of
them." Self-denial is shown not

> in literally bearing Christ's Cross, and living on locusts and wild
> honey, but in such light abstinences as come in our way, in some
> poor efforts at fasting and the like, in desiring to be poor rather
> than rich, solitary or lowly rather than well-connected, in living
> within our income, in avoiding display, in being suspicious of com-
> forts and luxuries; all of which are too trifling for the person obser-
> ving them to think about, yet have their use in proving and
> improving his heart.[73]

Self-denial is particularly useful as evidence of religious obedience. And if one had to define the authentic Christian in
terms of Newman's spirituality, one would be very tempted to
say he or she is the *obedient* Christian. This is not because obedience is more important than faith and love, but because it
is the concrete proof and realization of things more important
than itself, things only too easily corrupted or counterfeited.
As usual, Newman is realistic about the difficulties of obedience,
which "is very grievous to habitual sinners" even after they have
been converted. However, distrustful as he is about emotions

and feelings, he recognizes that in the early stages after conversion they are very useful in providing "an impulse which may
carry us over the first obstacles," leading us "to the more sober
and higher comfort resulting from that real *love* for religion,
which obedience itself will have by that time begun to form
in us, and will gradually go on to perfect." The "excitement
of mind" caused by a religious conversion "will wear away," but
it "may be made a means of leading [us] into a sound religious
course of life." "Therefore," Newman advises, "obey *promptly*;
make use of it while it lasts; it waits for no man."[74] Again, "obedience to God's commandments is ever easy, and almost without
effort to those who begin to serve Him from the beginning of
their days; whereas those who wait a while, find it grievous in
proportion to their delay." For God only "very gradually . . .
opens upon us the complicated duties of life," which "*would* be
grievous if put upon us all at once."[75] And obedience is so
difficult precisely because the effects of our past sins form bad
habits in us, although a person may not be "conscious of the
load of corrupt nature and sinful habits which hang upon his
will, and clog it in each particular exercise of it."[76] On the other
hand, continual obedience creates good habits which in turn
make obedience easier: "if we strove to obey God's will in all
things, we actually should be gradually training our hearts into
the fulness of a Christian spirit."[77] In other words, "We must
become what we are not; we must learn to love what we do
not love, and practise ourselves in what is difficult."[78] Like self-
denial, obedience in little things is especially important: "such
creatures are we, there is the most close and remarkable connexion between small observances and the permanence of our
chief habits and practices." In the same way disobedience begins
in "(apparently) slight omissions" and ends "in open unbelief."[79]
But it is "the observance of all lowly deeds of ordinary obedience"
which is "the most pleasing sacrifice to God."[80]

Obedience is also the best antidote to religious doubts and
problems: "To all those who are perplexed in any way soever,
who wish for light but cannot find it, one precept must be
given,—*obey*. It is obedience which brings a man into the right

path; it is obedience keeps him there and strengthens him in it." Moreover, by setting about "to obey God, in the ordinary businesses of daily life, we are at once interested by realities which withdraw our minds from vague fears and uncertain in-definite surmises about the future."[81] But obedience has a very positive as well as a negative importance, for "it is the rule of God's providence, that those who act up to their light, shall be rewarded with clearer light."[82] It is a spiritual point which Newman never tires of repeating and which is enshrined in his famous hymn "Lead, Kindly Light" in the words "one step enough for me":[83] "Act up to your light, though in the midst of difficulties, and you will be carried on, you do not know how far." For every "truth has its own order; we cannot join the way of life at any point of the course we please; we cannot learn advanced truths before we have learned primary ones. . . . but when men refuse to profit by light already granted, their light is turned to darkness."[84] As the Bible constantly teaches, "obe-dience to the light we possess is the way to gain more light."[85]

Nor must our obedience be anything other than uncondi-tional: "till we aim at complete, unreserved obedience in all things, we are not really Christians at all."[86] For "it is possible to be *generally* conscientious, or what the world calls honourable and high-principled, yet to be destitute of that religious fear and strictness, which God calls conscientiousness, but which the world calls superstition or narrowness of mind."[87] Thus most so-called conscientious people are concerned "not how to please God, but how to please themselves without displeasing Him." They simply "make this world the first object in their minds, and use religion as a corrective, a restraint, upon *too much* at-tachment to the world." They "do not take for the object towards which they act, God's will, but certain maxims, rules, or measures, right perhaps as far as they go, but defective because they admit of being subjected to certain other ultimate ends, which are not religious. . . . And thus they are what is popularly called moral, without being religious."[88]

And so we arrive at the conclusion that true obedience is impossible without religious faith: "Faith is the element of all perfection; he who begins with faith, will end in unspotted and entire holiness."[89] For "faith is itself of a holy nature, and the first fruits and earnest of holiness to come."[90] The fact is that faith and obedience are the same thing—"They are but one thing viewed differently." This is because to "believe is to look beyond this world to God, and to obey is to look beyond this world to God; to believe is of the heart, and to obey is of the heart; to believe is not a solitary act, but a consistent habit of trust; and to obey is not a solitary act, but a consistent habit of doing our duty in all things." Faith and obedience develop together: "In proportion as a man believes, so he obeys; they come together, and grow together, and last through life."[91]

One of the most consistent themes of Newman's preaching is the difficulty of consistency in the Christian life. So bad is "the scandal which a Christian's inconsistency brings upon his cause" that Newman can ask: "The Christian world, so called, what is it practically, but a witness for Satan rather than a witness for Christ? . . . is there any *antecedent* prejudice against religion so great as that which is occasioned by the lives of its professors?"[92] Part of the problem lies in the effect of changing circumstances: "We feel variously according to the place, time, and people we are with. We are serious on Sunday, and we sin deliberately on Monday."[93] The truth is "We can never answer how we shall act under new circumstances."[94] What is especially striking is that "if we look to some of the most eminent saints of Scripture, we shall find their recorded errors to have occurred in those parts of their duty in which each had had most trial, and generally showed obedience most perfect."[95] And the greatest of Christian saints "have exhibited inconsistencies such as to surprise and shock their most ardent disciples."[96] As for lesser Christians, "in the heart and life of even the better sort of men, that continual repentance must ever go hand in hand with our endeavours to obey."[97] "In all ages," then, "consistent obedience is a very rare endowment."[98] Much inconsistency is the involuntary result of past sins: "past years rise up against us in present offences; gross inconsistencies show themselves in our character."[99] It is to "single or forgotten sins" that "are not improbably to be traced the strange inconsistencies of character which we often witness in our experience of life."[100] So concerned is Newman with the importance of consistency that he even suggests that quantity is better than quality in the sense that someone "serves with a perfect heart, who serves God in all parts of his duty; and, not here and there, but here and there and everywhere; not perfectly indeed as regards the quality of his obedience, but perfectly as regards its extent; not completely, but consistently."[101] And so he can conclude: "The very test of a mature Christian, of a true saint, is consistency in all things."[102]

One very obvious kind of general inconsistency that Newman never tires of condemning is the disparity between what people profess and what they actually do. We like "to persuade ourselves, that to *feel* religiously, to confess our love of religion, and to be able to talk of religion, will stand in the place of careful obedience."[103] Our works do not keep pace with our words:

> He who does one little deed of obedience, whether he denies himself some comfort to relieve the sick and needy, or curbs his temper, or forgives an enemy, or asks forgiveness for an offence committed by him, or resists the clamour or ridicule of the world— such an one . . . evinces more true faith than could be shown by the most fluent religious conversation, the most intimate knowledge of Scripture doctrine, or the most remarkable agitation and change of religious sentiments. Yet how many are there who sit still with folded hands, dreaming, doing nothing at all, thinking they have done every thing, or need do nothing, when they merely have had these good *thoughts*, which will save no one![104]

For it is "easy to make professions, easy to say fine things in speech or in writing, easy to astonish men with truths which they do not know, and sentiments which rise above human nature," but "Let not your words run on; force every one of them into action. . . ."[105]

In short, "say nothing for saying's sake," but "do much and say little!"[106] After all, "he who does one deed of obedience for Christ's sake, let him have no imagination and no fine feeling, is a better man . . . than the most eloquent speaker, and the most sensitive hearer, of the glory of the Gospel, if such men do not practise up to their knowledge."[107] Feelings without corresponding actions are worse than useless: "God has made us feel in order that we may *go on to act* in consequence of feeling; if then we allow our feelings to be excited without acting upon them, we do mischief to the moral system within us, just as we might spoil a watch, or other piece of mechanism, by playing with the wheels of it. We weaken its springs, and they cease to act truly."[108] This is true particularly of those "vain talkers about philanthropy," who "usually show the emptiness of their profession, by being morose and cruel in the private relations of life, which they seem to account as subjects beneath their notice," but who

> talk magnificently about loving the whole human race with a comprehensive affection. . . . Such vaunting professions, what do they come to? that such men have certain benevolent *feelings* towards the world,—feelings and nothing more;—nothing more than unstable feelings, the mere offspring of an indulged imagination, which exist only when their minds are wrought upon, and are sure to fail them in the hour of need. This is not to love men, it is but to talk about love.—The real love of man *must* depend on practice.[109]

As Newman puts it in one of his memorable aphorisms: "That a thing is true, is no reason that it should be said, but that it should be done."[110] If we feel "the remorse and shame of a bad conscience" and make some "good resolution," we should "follow it up at once by *acting upon* it," otherwise we shall encourage "a habit of inattention and insensibility."[111]

Newman is convinced that spiritual progress depends on self-knowledge, without which, he argues, it is not possible even to understand "the great Christian doctrines." To say that we believe these doctrines without first understanding ourselves is to use "words without meaning":

For it is in proportion as we search our hearts and understand our own nature, that we understand what is meant by an Infinite Governor and Judge; in proportion as we comprehend the nature of disobedience and our actual sinfulness, that we feel what is the blessing of the removal of sin, redemption, pardon, sanctification, which otherwise are mere words.

If this is true, then "self-knowledge is at the root of all real religious knowledge."[112]

In order to have self-knowledge, it is essential, Newman insists, to practice self-examination. Merely "to speak of human nature as corrupt in the general" is not enough; we need to have "some true notion of the depths and deceitfulness of the heart."[113] But if "the office of self-examination lies rather in detecting what is bad in us than in ascertaining what is good," we also need to remember that in "contemplating our sins" we "keep Christ before us." After all, the "essence of Faith is to look out of ourselves," not to be imprisoned in one's "own thoughts." And Newman is emphatic that in recommending self-examination he is not advocating the kind of introspection ("a continual self-contemplation and reference to self") whereby one examines "the heart with a view of ascertaining whether it is in a spiritual state or no."[114] The "purpose of self-examination" is negative rather than positive; it is intended simply "to inform us of our sins" not of "our improvement."[115] One important purpose of self-examination is to draw a person's attention to "the number and variety of bad or foolish thoughts which he suffers, and dwells on in private, which he would be ashamed to put into words, and he will at once see, how very poor a test his outward demeanour in life is of his real holiness in the sight of God."[116] Essentially, self-examination brings to light the faults that are hidden from ourselves: "Conscience at first warns us against sin; but if we disregard it, it soon ceases to upbraid us; and thus sins, once known, in time become secret sins. It seems then . . . that the more guilty we are, the less we know it; for the oftener we sin, the less we are distressed at it."[117]

No preacher has ever explored with greater penetration and subtlety the ramifications of human sinfulness. Again and again, Newman fastens on the fecundity of single sins. Sinful thoughts lead very easily to sinful actions:

> Evil thoughts do us no harm, if recognized, if repelled, if protested against by the indignation and self-reproach of the mind. It is when we do not discern them, when we admit them, when we cherish them, that they ripen into principles.[118]

Sin is self-propagating: "When a man begins to do wrong, he cannot answer for himself how far he may be carried on. . . . One false step forces him to another, for retreat is impossible."[119] Once "we have begun an evil course, we cannot retrace our steps."[120] It is fortunate that we cannot realize the full implications of our sins: "Did we see the complete consequences of any one sin, did we see how it spreads by the contagion of example and influence through the world, how many souls it injures, and what its eternal effects are, doubtless we should become speechless and motionless, as though we saw the flames of hell fire."[121] Just as the sins of childhood imprint "indelible hues" on people's characters, so too

> when the mind is excited, thrown out of its ordinary state . . . as if into that original unformed state when it was more free to choose good and evil, then in like manner it takes impressions, and those indelible ones, and withal almost unconsciously, after the manner of childhood. This is one reason why a time of trial is often such a crisis in a man's spiritual history. It is a season when the iron is heated and malleable; one or two strokes serve to fashion it as a weapon for God or for Satan.

Single sins may also "account for the strange way in which defects of character are buried in a man," until "certain circumstances . . . bring them out." Again, "single sins indulged or neglected are often the cause of other defects of character, which seem to have no connexion with them, but which after all are rather systematic of the former, than themselves at the

bottom of the mischief." Everybody probably has "some beset-
ting sin or other, some infirmity, some temptation; and in
resisting this lies their trial." But, Newman points out, when
someone is "very religious *all but* this one infirmity," this same
"indulged infirmity may in consequence be producing most
distressing effects on his spiritual state . . . without his being
aware of it."[122] So many sins "have so grown into us as to become
part of us, and in which we now live, not knowing, or but partially knowing, that they are sins."[123]

Our great and only defense against sin lies in flight: "resist
the beginnings of evil, I do not mean the first act merely, but
the rising thought of evil. . . . Directly we are made aware
of the temptation, we shall, if we are wise, turn our backs upon
it, without waiting to think and reason about it; we shall engage
our mind in other thoughts." For at the beginning "our conscience tells us, in a plain straightforward way, what is right
and what is wrong; but when we trifle with this warning, our
reason becomes perverted, and comes in aid of our wishes, and
deceives us to our ruin."[124] Our voluntary sins lead to involuntary sins "which arise from our former habits of sin, though now
long abandoned," but which nevertheless give "a colour to our
thoughts, words, and works," so that our "former self clings"
to us, "as a poisoned garment, and eats into" us.

As a preacher, Newman is as severely denunciatory of sin
as he is keenly sensitive to the appalling difficulty for fallen
human beings to avoid sin. Indeed, he has to admit, "the process of learning to obey God is, in one sense, a process of sinning, from the nature of the case."[125] The struggle is constant,
but still not hopeless:

> Never suffer sin to remain upon you; let it not grow old in you;
> wipe it off while it is fresh, else it will stain; let it not get ingrained;
> let it not eat its way in, and rust in you. It is of a consuming nature;
> it is like a canker; it will eat your flesh.[126]

Asceticism

This account of Newman's view of the Christian life needs to be completed with a look at some other aspects and themes of the spirituality we find in the *Parochial and Plain Sermons*.

As we might expect from what has gone before, Newman's idea of the spiritual life is characterized by his disparagement of the dramatic and exciting. The importance of stability is particularly stressed: "Be on your guard especially, when you get into novel situations or circumstances which interest and delight you, lest they throw you out of your regularity in prayer. Any thing new or unexpected is dangerous to you." The great danger is to become "*unsettled*," when "stability of mind is the chief of virtues, for it is Faith."[127] Calmness, not excitement, is the hallmark of the mature Christian, although Newman certainly does not exclude legitimate outbreaks of emotion (which indeed are not in short supply in his own sermons):

> To be excited is not the *ordinary* state of the mind, but the extraordinary, the now and then state. . . . it *ought not* to be the common state of the mind; and if we are encouraging within us this excitement, this unceasing rush and alternation of feelings, and think that this, and this only, is being in earnest in religion, we are harming our minds, and (in one sense) I may even say grieving the peaceful Spirit of God, who would silently and tranquilly work His Divine work in our hearts.

Instead, we need to cultivate "still emotion, to calm us, to remind us what and where we are, to lead us to a purer and serener temper, and to that deep unruffled love of God and man."[128] The implication is that religious leaders, for example, are placed in a peculiarly invidious position that almost denies them the possibility of sanctity:

> There is a want of sympathy between much business and calm devotion, great splendour and a simple faith, which will be to no one more painful than to the Christian, to whom God has assigned some post of especial responsibility or distinction. To maintain

a religious spirit in the midst of engagements and excitements of this world is possible only to a saint.[129]

But far from inner calmness and tranquillity signifying inactivity, "the calmer our hearts, the more active be our lives; the more tranquil we are, the more busy; the more resigned, the more zealous; the more unruffled, the more fervent."[130]

The quiet rhythm of routine implies habits and, as we have seen, Newman emphasizes sharply this less than exciting aspect of the Christian life. Indeed, he goes so far as to define grace in terms of habit: "We do not know what we mean by a habit, except as a state or quality of mind *under* which we act in this or that particular way; it is a permanent power in the mind; and what is grace but this?" But whereas "grace was to [Adam] instead of a habit," fallen man has to gain it "by dint of exercise, working up towards it by religious acts."[131] Our responsibility, then, is to make sure that we perform the right actions which will create the right habits: "We have power over our deeds . . . we have no direct power over our habits. Let us but secure our actions . . . and our habits will follow."[132]

The unexciting, traditional Christian ascetic practices are also strongly recommended. But it is important to note that fasting, for instance, is not encouraged simply as a penance but rather as related to Christian love, which "is quenched and extinguished by self-indulgence, and cherished by self-denial . . . for sensual living hardens the heart, while abstinence softens and refines it." We may "dispense with fasting," but then we "may neglect also to cultivate love." For we have to learn to "live a life, not of sense, but of spirit."[133] It is remarkable how Newman insists on what may strike many as an unlikely connection: "Is it wonderful that we have no love, when we neglect altogether that great ordinance whereby love is nurtured, abstinence and fasting?"[134] Not that Newman is not careful to warn of the spiritual danger of ascetic practices like fasting, since "in some wonderful unknown way they open the next world for good and evil upon us, and are an introduction to somewhat of an extraordinary conflict with the powers of evil."[135]

Moreover, a very practical spiritual rule applies to fasting as to other devotions: "We ought to attempt nothing but what we can do." We ought also to "guard against a reaction" by not, for example, eating to excess after fasting.[136]

However, ascetic practices are also important because they detach us from this world, which "is sweet to the lips, but bitter to the taste. It pleases at first, but not at last." Not intended to be seen, they also remind us of the cross of Christ, which "though it be the true interpretation of this world, is not prominently manifested in it, upon its surface, but is concealed; so again, when received into the faithful heart, there it abides as a living principle, but deep, and hidden from observation." Thus observances like fasting help us to attain a right balance between the things of this world and the next world, as Newman explains in a superbly succinct passage:

> They alone are able truly to enjoy this world, who begin with the world unseen. They alone enjoy it, who have first abstained from it. They alone can truly feast, who have first fasted; they alone are able to use the world, who have learned not to abuse it; they alone inherit it, who take it as a shadow of the world to come, and who for that world to come relinquish it.[137]

In spite of his overpowering sense of the power of sin, Newman is not as pessimistic about the possibility of spiritual progress as may seem. He once preached, "Who can say the heights to which in time men can proceed in all things, who beginning by little and little, yet in the distance shadow forth great things?"[138] But we must "begin with the beginning" and not "*with* the end," for we have to "mount up the heavenly ladder step by step."[139] And so we shall make progress, imperceptible though it may be:

> It is by going on quietly and steadily, with the thought of Him in our mind's eye, that by little and little we shall gain something of warmth, light, life, and love. We shall not perceive ourselves changing. It will be like the unfolding of leaves in spring.[140]

And we shall succeed not in spite of but through our failures:

We advance to the truth by experience of error; we succeed through failures. We know not how to do right except by having done wrong. . . . Such is the process by which we succeed; we walk to heaven backward.[141]

To fail from a worldly point of view is to succeed spiritually, for there is "a mysterious connexion between real advancement and self-abasement," whereby we find ourselves "as by a divine charm, getting power over the world and rising among the creatures."[142] Indeed, "the good cannot conquer, except by suffering."[143]

At the heart of Newman's spirituality is the doctrine of self-abandonment—"a surrender of ourselves, soul and body, to Him."[144] We are called to admit Christ into the "shrine" of our hearts so that he is "that true and better self, of which self itself should be but an instrument and minister," and not to keep "a self where God is not."[145] "The one thing, which is all in all to us, is to live in Christ's presence; to hear His voice, to see His countenance."[146]

In order to try to live in Christ's presence, one must, of course, pray, for prayer is "*divine* converse." Not to pray is not to "claim" one's "citizenship with heaven." Apart from having "a *natural* effect, in spiritualizing and elevating the soul," prayer makes "the next world" a "reality" to the Christian.[147]

> Prayer and fasting are the so-called wings of the soul, and they who neither fast nor pray, cannot follow Christ. They cannot lift up their hearts to Him. They have no treasure above, but their treasure, and their heart, and their faculties are all upon the earth; the earth is their portion, and not heaven.[148]

It would be impossible for Newman to talk about prayer without referring to the indwelling of the Holy Spirit: since we are, in the words of St. Paul, temples of the Holy Spirit, our prayer is really the work of the Holy Spirit. But prayer of course also reveals to us the fact that the Spirit is present in us: for "as our bodily life discovers itself by its activity, so is the presence of the Holy Spirit in us discovered by a spiritual activity; and this activity is the spirit of continual prayer. Prayer is to spiritual life what the beating of the pulse and the drawing of the breath are to the life of the body."[149] The reason contemplative prayer does not come naturally to us is that the fall has deprived us of "man's happiness in Paradise, not to think about himself or to be conscious of himself"—"for what is contemplation but a resting in the thought of God to the forgetfulness of self?"[150] And Newman urges the importance of meditation, of "thinking habitually and constantly of Him and of His deeds and sufferings. . . . And by this, and nothing short of this, will our hearts come to feel as they ought." It is through prayer that we receive the spirit of holiness, Newman explains with a striking image:

> We have stony hearts, hearts as hard as the highways; the history of Christ makes no impression on them. And yet, if we would be saved, we must have tender, sensitive, living hearts; our hearts must be broken, must be broken up like ground, and dug, and watered, and tended, and cultivated, till they become as gardens, gardens of Eden, acceptable to our God, gardens in which the Lord God may walk and dwell.[151]

Like holiness, prayer is not just for a Christian elite: "holding communion with God, or living in God's sight . . . may be done all through the day, wherever we are, and is commanded us as the duty, or rather the characteristic, of those who are really servants and friends of Jesus Christ."[152]

Newman does not attempt to disguise the difficulty of prayer, "because our thoughts are so apt to wander."[153] Certainly it is easy to pray if that simply means "a rush of feelings"; but "it is not at all easy to be in the habit day after day and hour after hour, in all frames of mind, and under all outward circumstances, to bring before God a calm, collected, awakened soul."[154] It involves a real self-sacrifice, and Newman again emphasizes the need for regularity, for "certain *times* for private prayer, over and above the secret thought of God which must ever be alive in us." For, if we leave religion as a subject of thought for all hours of the day equally, it will be thought of in none. In all things it is by small beginnings and appointed channels that an advance is made to extensive works. Stated times of prayer put us in that posture . . . in which we ought ever to be; they urge us forward in a heavenly direction, and then the stream carries us on.

There is another reason for regularity in our prayer life: it is "a principal means of reminding" us that "spiritual life is obedience . . . not a mere feeling or a taste." Again, Jesus told us to pray for our "daily bread"; but "if you have not prayed for it this morning, it will profit you little that you prayed for it yesterday. You did then pray and you obtained,—but not a supply for two days." Newman warns solemnly that we "gradually become weaker without knowing it" as a result of omitting our daily prayers.[155]

As well as set times, he recommends set forms for verbal prayer rather than praying "at random" with whatever words happen to come to mind. He gives several reasons: first, "to avoid the irreverence of many or unfit words and rude half-religious thoughts, it is necessary to pray from book or memory"; second, it is "necessary to guard us against the irreverence of *wandering* thoughts"; third, they are "useful in securing us from the irreverence of *excited thoughts*." Of course, Newman is reacting against an emotional Evangelicalism, much given to extempore prayer, and is anxious to discourage the "excitement" of "unceasing rush and alternation of feelings." The prohibition of informal prayer may seem to us somewhat excessive, but Newman has a perfectly valid point in wanting a spirituality intended "to keep us from self-willed earnestness, to still emotion, to calm us, to remind us what and where we are, to lead us to a purer and serener temper, and to that deep unruffled love of God and man, which is really the fulfilling of the law, and the perfection of human nature." For this purpose, he recommends "calm, composed, and short" prayers rather than ones "written in strong and impassioned language." There is a fourth reason for formal, set prayers: they "teach those who pray poorly to pray better," for "the power of praying, being a habit, must be acquired, like all other habits, by practice."[156] Finally, set prayers are an aid to the memory of the Christian in all the circumstances of life, and may indeed be invaluable at certain times of crisis.

Newman goes out of his way to recommend praying for others. "Intercession," he says, "is the characteristic of Christian worship, the privilege of the heavenly adoption, the exercise of the perfect and spiritual mind." Since Christianity is a "social religion" and involves Christians praying together, "united prayer is necessarily of an intercessory character, as being offered for each other and for the whole, and for self as one of the whole." But there is a theological reason why the prayer of a Christian must be profoundly intercessory: "He is made after the pattern and in the fulness of Christ—he is what Christ is. Christ intercedes above, and he intercedes below."[157]

No account of the Christian life can ignore the problem of suffering. And before we turn in the final chapter of this book to look at what Newman has to say about death and the afterlife, we conclude this chapter, appropriately, with a consideration of his approach to suffering in his pastoral preaching. He leaves us in no doubt that suffering is an almost essential part of the Christian Life: "to approach Him has been, from the first, to be partaker, more or less, in His sufferings; I do not say in the case of every individual who believes in Him, but as regards the more conspicuous, the more favoured, His choice instruments, and His most active servants." It is certainly a "great privilege . . . that all pain and trouble, borne in faith and patience, will be accounted as marks of Christ." Christianity, therefore, has turned "a punishment into a privilege, in the case of all pain, and especially of bodily pain, which is the most mysterious of all." True, "it has no sanctifying influence in itself. Bad men are made worse by it." Indeed, it can have "a strong tendency to do our souls harm, viz., by making us selfish." For the "natural effect . . . of pain and fear, is to individualize us in our own minds, to fix our thoughts on ourselves, to make us selfish." Suffering, then, "arrests us: . . . it puts, as it were, a finger upon us to ascertain for us our own individuality. But it does no more than this; if such a warning does not lead us through the stirrings of our conscience heavenwards, it does but imprison us in ourselves and make us selfish." But pain, "which by nature leads us only to ourselves, carries on the Christian mind from the thought of self to the contemplation of Christ . . . and, while we gaze upon Him, we learn to forget ourselves." Moreover, "Who is there but must own that with Christ's sufferings before us, pain and tribulation are, after all, not only the most blessed, but even the most congruous attendants upon those who are called to inherit the benefit of them?"[158]

Newman's sense that suffering is a sign of God's love is no mere pious rhetoric. He warns almost fiercely, "Be sure of this: that if He has any love for you, if He sees aught of good in your soul, *He* will afflict you, if you will not afflict yourselves. He will not let you escape."[159] The fact is, without suffering holiness is practically impossible, for "nothing short of suffering, except in rare cases, makes us what we should be."[160] As he explains more generally in another sermon, "If there were no enemy, there could be no conflict; were there no trouble, there could be no faith; were there no trial, there could be no love; were there no fear, there could be no hope. Hope, faith, and love are weapons, and weapons imply foes and encounters."[161] Without suffering, "men, though men, are like spoilt children," whereas somebody "who has been long under the rod of God, becomes God's possession." Suffering has the particular benefit of making us sympathetic to others—"consecrated by affliction as a minister of God's mercies to the afflicted." For "to comfort well we must first be afflicted ourselves."[162] Finally, suffering should be seen as the penance for sin—"How do you know, but that, if you will not satisfy the debt of daily sin now, it will hereafter come upon you with interest?"[163]

8

LIFE AFTER DEATH

The Anglican Sermons

We began this book with an account of Newman's theology of faith. We shall end it with an exposition of his eschatology, that is, his theology of life after death, to which faith looks forward and in which faith finds its fulfillment.

As an Anglican, Newman preached that this life, quite apart from revelation, seems to imply another life after death, if only because "we are ever expecting great things from life, from our internal consciousness every moment of our having souls; and we are ever being disappointed." And so our "earthly life . . . gives promise of what it does not accomplish. It promises immortality, yet it is mortal." The unfulfilled potential of this life seems to demand fulfillment in another life:

> The very greatness of our powers makes this life look pitiful; the very pitifulness of this life forces on our thoughts to another; and the prospect of another gives a dignity and value to this life which promises it; and thus this life is at once great and little, and we rightly condemn it while we exalt its importance.

This is true not only of our abilities and talents, but also and more importantly of our moral and spiritual powers:

There is something in moral truth and goodness, in faith, in firmness, in heavenly-mindedness, in meekness, in courage, in loving-kindness, to which this world's circumstances are quite unequal, for which the longest life is insufficient, which makes the highest opportunities of this world disappointing, which must burst the prison of this world to have its appropriate range.[1]

But if the potentiality of this life seems to be unrealized, the existence of a life to come opens up undreamed of possibilities, the "wonderful things of the new world":

Who can express the surprise and rapture which will come upon those, who then at last apprehend them for the first time, and to whose perceptions they are new! Who can imagine by a stretch of fancy the feelings of those who having died in faith, wake up to enjoyment![2]

In simpler psychological terms, Newman imagines the "most transporting" feeling which will

come over the soul of the faithful Christian, when just separated from the body, and conscious that his trial is once for all over. Though his life has been a long and painful discipline, yet when it is over, we may suppose him to feel at the moment the same sort of surprise at its being ended, as generally follows any exertion in this life, when the object is gained and the anticipation over.[3]

When we die we shall also see God as he really is. This will not be a shock or surprise to holy people, but it will be to the ordinary sinful run of humanity. Most people "begin to lose sight of God" in this life through sinning:

Like men who fall asleep, the real prospect still flits before them in their dreams, but out of shape and proportion, discoloured, crowded with all manner of fancies and untruths; and so they proceed in that dream of sin, more or less profound. . . . Death alone gives lively perceptions to the generality of men, who then see the very truth, such as they saw it before they began to sin, but more clear and more fearful.[4]

When we die we come before God as our judge, and the prospect of that encounter fills us with fear, if only because, as Newman depicts it in his incomparable prose, the meeting will be a profoundly personal one:

> We are not merely to be rewarded or punished, we are to be judged. Recompense is to come upon our actions, not by a mere general provision or course of nature, as it does at present, but from the Lawgiver himself in person. We have to stand before His righteous Presence, and that one by one. One by one we shall have to endure His holy and searching eye. At present we are in a world of shadows. What we see is not substantial. Suddenly it will be rent in twain and vanish away, and our Maker will appear. And then, I say, that first appearance will be nothing less than a personal intercourse between the Creator and every creature. He will look on us, while we look on Him.[5]

The fearful simplicity of that last sentence does not belie the love of God, for, as we shall see, the dread nature of the judgment lies in the fact that it is the searching glance of Love itself which is the judgment.

Unlike our own death which comes closer every day, the last judgment and Christ's second coming are no nearer and no further away than when Christ left the world, which is not moving

> towards the end, but along it, and on the brink of it; and is at all times equally near that great event, which, did it run towards, it would at once run into. Christ, then, is ever at our doors; as near eighteen hundred years ago as now, and not nearer now than then; and not nearer when He comes than now. When He says that He will come soon, "soon" is not a word of time, but of natural order. This present state of things . . . is ever *close upon* the next world, and resolves itself into it. As when a man is given over, he may die any moment, yet lingers; as an implement of war may any moment explode, and must at some time; as we listen for a clock to strike, and at length it surprises us; as a crumbling arch hangs, we know not how, and is not safe to pass under; so creeps

on this feeble weary world, and one day, before we know where we are, it will end.

Newman explains that the Gospels do not recognize any temporal interval between Christ's first coming, as a result of which "the last time" has already come, and his second coming, since it is only "as it were, an accident." For Christians, Christ is ever "just coming, *all but* come."[6]

The Catholic Church teaches that the soul has three possible destinations after death: heaven, hell, or purgatory. All three possibilities are to be found in the eschatology of Newman's Anglican sermons. The fact that heaven and hell feature in his preaching is no surprise, but Newman found himself compelled to allow for a purification after death which closely resembles the Catholic purgatory.

The traditional idea that heaven "is a certain place, and not a mere state" is justified in Newman's eyes by the doctrine of the ascension of Christ "to the right hand of God."[7] On the other hand, he insists on the mistake of supposing heaven to be "a place like this earth; I mean, a place where every one may choose and take his *own* pleasure." Far from heaven being such a place, if an irreligious person "were admitted into heaven, doubtless he would sustain a great disappointment." Not only would such a person be disappointed, but he would be excruciatingly unhappy:

> he could not *bear* the face of the Living God; the Holy God would be no object of joy to him. . . . None but the holy one can look upon the Holy One; without holiness no man can endure to see the Lord.

The fact is that "holiness, or inward separation from the world, is necessary to our admission into heaven, because heaven is *not* heaven, is not a place of happiness *except* to the holy." It is not hard to find analogies:

> There are bodily indispositions which affect the taste, so that the sweetest flavours become ungrateful to the palate; and indispositions which impair the sight, tinging the fair face of nature with

some sickly hue. In like manner, there is a moral malady which disorders the inward sight and taste; and no man labouring under it is in a condition to enjoy what Scripture calls 'the fulness of joy in God's presence, and pleasures at His right hand for evermore.'

So far from heaven being a source of happiness for the sinful, "Heaven would be hell to an irreligious man," for "if we wished to imagine a punishment for an unholy, reprobate soul, we perhaps could not fancy a greater than to *summon it to heaven*."[8]

Newman comes very close indeed to dissolving the distinction between heaven and hell, in the sense that hell for the unrepentant sinner is simply to be in heaven. Again he uses an analogy to suggest, not without a certain ironic amusement, how such a person would feel if he found himself in heaven:

> We know how unhappy we are apt to feel at present, when alone in the midst of strangers, or of men of different tastes and habits from ourselves. How miserable, for example, would it be to have to live in a foreign land, among a people whose faces we never saw before, and whose language we could not learn. And this is but a faint illustration of the loneliness of a man of earthly dispositions and tastes, thrust into the society of saints and angels. How forlorn would he wander through the courts of heaven! He would find no one like himself; he would see in every direction the marks of God's holiness, and these would make him shudder. He would feel himself always in His presence. He could no longer turn his thoughts another way, as he does now, when conscience reproaches him. He would know that the Eternal Eye was ever upon him; and that Eye of holiness, which is joy and life to holy creatures, would seem to him an Eye of wrath and punishment. God cannot change His nature. Holy He must ever be. But while He is holy, no unholy soul can be happy in heaven. Fire does not inflame iron, but it inflames straw. It would cease to be fire if it did not. And so heaven itself would be fire to those, who would fain escape across the great gulf from the torments of hell.[9]

In another sermon, however, Newman suggests that "a bad man, if brought to heaven, would not know he was in heaven," although he does not consider the further question whether, "on the contrary, the very fact of his being in heaven with all his unholiness upon him, would not be a literal torment to him, and light up the fires of hell within him."[10] Just as the extent of human suffering is commensurate with the degree to which we are conscious of it, so, Newman argues, the pain of hell involves the kind of acute awareness of our state, a concentrated consciousness we are able to avoid in this life. The damned can find no respite in "the dry apathy in which unbelievers on earth take refuge." Nor is any comfort to be found in "fatalism": "The devils see their doom was their own fault, yet they are unable to be sorry for it. It is their *will* that is in direct energetic variance with the will of God, and they know it."[11]

The Anglican Newman can sometimes sound as if there is no question of any other possibility after death apart from heaven or hell, "so that every person we meet is in God's unerring eye either on the one side or the other, and did He please to take him hence at once, would find himself either in paradise or in the place of torment."[12] But he also recognizes that there are people who may be saved but who are not yet sufficiently holy "to *do Him service in heaven.*"[13] And, in a remarkable anticipation of the modern Catholic theology of purgatory, he remarks in one sermon, "Doubtless we must all endure that fierce and terrifying vision of our real selves, that last fiery trial of the soul before its acceptance, a spiritual agony and second death to all who are not then supported by the strength of Him who died to bring them safe through it, and in whom on earth they have believed."[14] It is hard to see what else this purifying and sanctifying experience can be except purgatory.

Elsewhere Newman refuses to accept the belief that "after this life the souls of Christians ordinarily go into a prison called Purgatory, where they are kept in fire or other torment, till, their sins being burned away, they are at length fitted for that glorious kingdom into which nothing defiled can enter." He argues that neither the Bible nor tradition requires Anglicans to believe in this "very sad and depressing prospect."[15] But in the very same sermon he allows that the "Intermediate State" between death and the last judgment, when souls remain "for a season at a distance from heaven," may serve the very purpose of giving "time for growing in all holy things, and perfecting the inward development of the good seed sown in their hearts." For there are many people who "are very dark and feeble in their religious state, when they depart hence, though true servants of God as far as they go." The "time of waiting between death and Christ's coming," therefore, "may be profitable to those who have been His true servants here" as "a school-time of contemplation, as this world is a discipline of active service." Newman seems here to envisage this state before the resurrection of the dead as common to all, "a state which comes short of the glory which shall be revealed in us after the Resurrection, a state of waiting, meditation, hope, in which what has been sown on earth may be matured and completed." But unlike what he takes to be the purgatory of Roman Catholicism, it is "a state of repose, rest, security . . . a state more like paradise than heaven." However, again, he seems to advocate something very like praying for the dead when he asks, "Can the tyranny of earth hinder our holding a blessed and ever-enduring fellowship with those who are dead . . . ?"[16]

The Catholic Writings

When he wrote about the afterlife as a Catholic, Newman tried to give a fresh spiritual significance to the traditional doctrines. When the pagan Greek heroine of his novel *Callista* objects to the idea of hell, she is told that a life after death without the God of Christianity would be a virtual hell, for you "will still be the same being, but deprived of those outward stays and reliefs and solaces, which, such as they are, you now enjoy. You will be yourself, shut up in yourself." The relentless concentration on self, without the respite of any distraction, is the essence of Newman's hell, and as a kind of psychological explanation it strikes a remarkably modern note.

Assuming, then, first, that the soul always needs external objects to rest upon; next, that it has no prospect of any such when it leaves this visible scene; and thirdly, that the hunger and thirst, the gnawing of the heart, where it occurs, is as keen and piercing as a flame; it will follow there is nothing irrational in the notion of an eternal Tartarus.[17]

For centuries the existence of hell had been taken for granted by Christians, who, far from experiencing it as a problem for religious belief, usually imagined it in the crudest physical terms. But for nineteenth-century believers, confronted by new objections to Christianity raised by the rise of secular humanism, the doctrine of hell posed a special difficulty. Apart from understanding the doctrine in a spiritual way, Newman sought to alleviate the terribleness of everlasting damnation, an idea which seemed increasingly to cast doubt on the credibility of faith in a God of love. In the *Grammar of Assent* he suggests that what is meant by "eternal" punishment is not as obvious as it may appear:

Eternity, or endlessness, is in itself mainly a negative idea, though the idea of suffering is positive. Its fearful force, as an element of future punishment, lies in what it excludes; it means never any change of state, no annihilation or restoration; but what, considered positively, it adds to suffering, we do not know. For what we know, the suffering of one moment may in itself have no bearing, or but a partial bearing, on the suffering of the next; and thus, as far as its intensity is concerned, it may vary with every lost soul. This may be so, unless we assume that the suffering is necessarily attended by a consciousness of duration and succession, by a present imagination of its past and its future, by a sustained power of realizing its continuity.

And in a note on this passage, he tells the "story . . . of the monk, who, going out into the wood to meditate, was detained there by the song of a bird for three hundred years, which to his consciousness passed as only one hour."[18] The idea that pain essentially consists in the consciousness of its duration was an idea he had already fruitfully applied to the sufferings of Christ on the cross; the difference here is that it is used to minimize rather than maximize the punishment of hell. Damnation, too, without pain might be a possibility, or the pain might diminish in time. At least the Catholic doctrine of purgatory, which implied that there were "innumerable degrees of grace and sanctity among the saved,"[19] meant that there was a less awful alternative to hell. But Newman rejected the suggestion that the possibility of salvation might be extended beyond death, if only because this would presumably involve the period of probation being extended for all, including those who had already been saved in this life.

Newman's most extended piece of writing on the afterlife is his poem *The Dream of Gerontius*, made famous by Edward Elgar's oratorio. There Newman tries to convey the idea of disembodied souls in purgatory awaiting the final resurrection through a piercingly physical parallel:

> Hast thou not heard of those, who after loss
> Of hand or foot, still cried that they had pains
> In hand or foot, as though they had it still?
> So is it now with thee, who hast not lost
> Thy hand or foot, but all which made up man.

But the actual pain of purgatory is both intensified and justified in terms not of material fire but of God's spiritual love:

> It is the face of the Incarnate God
> Shall smite thee with that keen and subtle pain;
> And yet the memory which it leaves will be
> A sovereign febrifuge to heal the wound;
> And yet withal it will the wound provoke,
> And aggravate and widen it the more.

A doctrine which was popularly conceived of in crudely physical terms is again, like the concept of hell, realized by Newman as a supremely spiritual reality. The purgatorial pain will not be a punishment externally inflicted by God, but rather the pain and the punishment will be the sight of the loving God contrasted with the sight of one's own sinfulness:

> There is a pleading in His pensive eyes
> Will pierce thee to the quick, and trouble thee.
> And thou wilt hate and loathe thyself; for, though
> Now sinless, thou wilt feel that thou hast sinn'd,
> As never thou didst feel; and wilt desire
> To slink away, and hide thee from His sight:
> And yet wilt have a longing aye to dwell
> Within the beauty of His countenance.
> And these two pains, so counter and so keen,—
> The longing for Him, when thou seest Him not;
> The shame of self at thought of seeing Him,—
> Will be the veriest, sharpest purgatory.

Thus it is not so much pity as envy that is suggested by Gerontius's purgatory, the contradictory nature of which is evoked in a superbly concentrated and poised image—

> O happy, suffering soul! for it is safe,
> Consumed, yet quicken'd, by the glance of God.

And so the soul of Gerontius begins its final prayer with the poignantly paradoxical couplet

> Take me away, and in the lowest deep
> There let me be . . . [20]

Far from the pain of purgatory being feared, it is this very pain which the soul above all desires, for it is none other than a keen longing for God combined with a sense of utter unworthiness.

This demythologizing and discovery of the true significance of a doctrine which had been widely misunderstood and trivialized is only one of the many ways in which Newman's realization of the Christian faith anticipates the later rediscoveries of twentieth-century Catholic theologians who have returned to the scriptural and patristic sources of the tradition. And the possibility, of course, of recovering the wholeness of the gospel of Christ in the categories and terms of primitive Christianity rather than in the thought-forms of late medieval Scholasticism, in which both Reformation and Counter-Reformation have their roots, has enormous implications for the achievement of Christian unity.

ABBREVIATIONS

Newman collected his works in a uniform edition of 36 vols. (1868–81). Until his death in 1890 he continued making minor textual changes in reprints of individual volumes in this edition, of which all the volumes from 1886 were published by Longmans, Green, and Co. of London. References are usually to volumes in the uniform edition published after 1890 by Longmans, which are distinguished from other editions by not including publication details in parentheses after the title.

Apo.   *Apologia pro Vita Sua*, ed. Martin J. Svaglic (Oxford: Clarendon Press, 1967)
Ari.   *The Arians of the Fourth Century*
AW   *John Henry Newman: Autobiographical Writings*, ed. Henry Tristram (London and New York: Sheed and Ward, 1956)
Call.   *Callista: A Tale of the Third Century*
Cons.   *On Consulting the Faithful in Matters of Doctrine*, ed. John Coulson (London: Geoffrey Chapman, 1961)
DA   *Discussions and Arguments on Various Subjects*
Dev.   *An Essay on the Development of Christian Doctrine*
Diff. i, ii   *Certain Difficulties felt by Anglicans in Catholic Teaching*, 2 vols.
Ess. i, ii   *Essays Critical and Historical*, 2 vols.
GA   *An Essay in Aid of a Grammar of Assent*, ed. I. T. Ker (Oxford: Clarendon Press, 1985)
HS i, ii, iii   *Historical Sketches*, 3 vols.
Idea   *The Idea of a University*, ed. I. T. Ker (Oxford: Clarendon Press, 1976)
Jfc.   *Lectures on the Doctrine of Justification*

LD i–vi, xi–xxxi	The Letters and Diaries of John Henry Newman, ed. Charles Stephen Dessain et al., vols. i–vi (Oxford: Clarendon Press, 1978–84), xi–xxii (London: Nelson, 1961–72), xxiii-xxxi (Oxford: Clarendon Press, 1973–77)
LG	Loss and Gain: The Story of a Convert
Mix.	Discourses addressed to Mixed Congregations
OS	Sermons preached on Various Occasions
PS i–viii	Parochial and Plain Sermons, 8 vols.
Phil.N. i, ii	The Philosophical Notebook of John Henry Newman, ed. Edward Sillem, 2 vols. (Louvain: Nauwelaerts, 1969–70)
Prepos.	Present Position of Catholics in England
TP i	The Theological Papers of John Henry Newman on Faith and Certainty, ed. Hugo M. de Achaval, SJ, and J. Derek Holmes (Oxford: Clarendon Press, 1976)
TP ii	The Theological Papers of John Henry Newman on Biblical Inspiration and on Infallibility, ed. J. Derek Holmes (Oxford: Clarendon Press, 1979)
US	Fifteen Sermons preached before the University of Oxford
VM i, ii	The Via Media, 2 vols.
VV	Verses on Various Occasions

NOTES

1. Faith

1. *LD* i. 219, 226.
2. *DA* 295.
3. *Prepos.* 283–84.
4. *US* 177, 179, 182–84, 187–88, 190–93, 197–200.
5. *US* 203–4, 207, 209, 211–13, 215, 218.
6. *US* 224–28, 230, 232–34, 236, 239, 249–50.
7. *US* 253–56, 262, 267, 271–72, 274, 276, 266.
8. *LD* xi. 293; xv. 381.
9. *Apo.* 31.
10. *Dev.* 107, 123, 115, 327.
11. *LD* xi. 289.
12. *LD* xv. 457–58.
13. *LD* xix. 460.
14. *LD* xxi. 146.
15. *LD* xxiv. 146.
16. *GA* 187, 189–90.
17. *GA* 195–96, 202.
18. *LD* xxiv. 275–76.
19. *GA* 205–8.
20. *GA* 221, 223, 226, 232–33, 245.
21. *GA* 264, 266.
22. *GA* 253, 272, 274, 276–77, 299, 313.
23. *PS* viii. 188, 114.

2. Revelation

1. *Apo.* 36.
2. *Ari.* 80–82.

3. *Ari.* 84.
4. *Ess.* ii. 231–32.
5. *GA* 250.
6. *LD* xxviii. 257.
7. *US* 18, 23.
8. *PS* ii. 18.
9. *Call.* 314–15.
10. *GA* 72, 76, 251, 252.
11. *DA* 388.
12. *US* 330.
13. *DA* 130–31, 134.
14. *DA* 296.
15. *Diff.* ii. 236.
16. *Ari.* 36–37.
17. *Apo.* 36–37.
18. *Ari.* 145–46.
19. *Ess.* i. 41–42.
20. *Jfc.* 316.
21. *US* 331–32, 336.
22. *GA* 82–83.
23. *LD* xxiii. 99–100.
24. *LD* xxiii. 105.
25. *LD* xxv. 418.
26. *Diff.* ii. 236, 322.
27. *Ari.* 50–51.
28. *LD* v. 166.
29. *VM* i. 26–27, 245, 28, 244.
30. *DA* 146–48, 150–51.
31. *Diff.* ii. 12.
32. *US* 316–18, 320–1, 323.
33. *Dev.* 29, 5.
34. *Dev.* 34–36, 38–40.
35. *Dev.* 55–56, 58, 60, 62, 64–66, 68.
36. *Dev.* 79–80, 88–90, 92.
37. *Dev.* 93, 95, 97–98.
38. *Dev.* 100.
39. "Notes" is the more cautious, less definite word he uses in the revised second edition, although the word "test" is still to be found there.

40. *Dev.* 169–71.
41. *LD* xxiii. 288; xxiv. 325.

3. Redemption

1. *Dev.* 35–36, 324.
2. *Ess.* i. 47.
3. For a good defense of Newman's Christology, see Roderick Strange, "Newman and the Mystery of Christ," in Ian Ker and Alan G. Hill, eds., *Newman after a Hundred Years* (Oxford: Clarendon Press, 1990), 323-36.
4. *Ess.* i. 74.
5. *PS* iii. 156–57.
6. *PS* v. 93, 118.
7. *PS* ii. 32.
8. *PS* ii. 39–40.
9. *Mix.* 321–22, 358.
10. *PS* iii. 170.
11. *PS* vi. 58.
12. *PS* i. 207.
13. *PS* ii. 211.
14. *PS* vi. 90.
15. *Ari.* 46.
16. *LD* v. 45.
17. *PS* vi. 89.
18. *PS* vi. 79.
19. *US* 118.
20. *Mix.* 306–8, 310–11.
21. *Ess.* i. 67.
22. *Mix.* 326–29.
23. *Mix.* 329, 331, 334–35, 341.
24. *Ess.* i. 247.
25. *Jfc.* 174.
26. *Jfc.* 222.
27. *PS* i. 285–86, 290.
28. *PS* i. 176.
29. *PS* ii. 39.
30. *PS* ii. 142–43.
31. *PS* ii. 221.

32. *PS* ii. 222.
33. *PS* ii. 229.
34. *PS* iv. 248–49.
35. *PS* v. 138–39.
36. *PS* vi. 124, 126.
37. *PS* iv. 168.
38. *PS* v. 156–58.
39. *PS* v. 156–58, 161.
40. *PS* v. 181.
41. *PS* vi. 175–76, 184.
42. *PS* v. 171.
43. *Jfc.* 2.
44. *Jfc.* 8–9.
45. *Jfc.* 11–13.
46. *Jfc.* 19.
47. *Jfc.* 21.
48. *Jfc.* 23.
49. *Jfc.* 24.
50. *Jfc.* 26.
51. *Jfc.* 27–28.
52. *Jfc.* 30–31, 34.
53. *Jfc.* 36–37, 61.
54. *Jfc.* 56.
55. *Jfc.* 263–66.
56. *Jfc.* 65.
57. *Jfc.* 72–73.
58. *Jfc.* 78.
59. *Jfc.* 81.
60. *Jfc.* 96, 99, 174.
61. *Jfc.* 136–38.
62. *Jfc.* 154.
63. *Jfc.* 243, 303, 266.

4. Mary

1. *PS* ii. 132–36.
2. *PS* ii. 132.
3. *PS* vi. 285.
4. *PS* ii. 31–32.

5. *PS* ii. 129.
6. *PS* iv. 341.
7. *Mix.* 350–51.
8. *Mix.* 352, 354, 369.
9. *Mix.* 371–72, 361.
10. *Diff.* ii. 28.
11. *Diff.* ii. 87–88.
12. *Diff.* ii. 31–32.
13. *Diff.* ii. 35–36.
14. *Diff.* ii. 45–46.
15. *Diff.* ii. 46–49.
16. *Diff.* ii. 54–55.
17. *Diff.* ii. 58–59.
18. *Diff.* ii. 62.
19. *Diff.* ii. 73.
20. *Diff.* ii. 105–6.
21. *Diff.* ii. 92–93.

5. Church

1. *PS* i. 153–54.
2. *PS* ii. 66.
3. *PS* ii. 391.
4. *PS* vi. 313–14.
5. *PS* vii. 236–37.
6. *PS* iii. 207, 222, 224; v. 41.
7. *PS* iii. 270.
8. *PS* iv. 170, 174, 171.
9. *PS* iii. 191, 202.
10. *PS* vii. 231.
11. *PS* vii. 232–33.
12. *PS* iv. 169.
13. *PS* ii. 391.
14. *PS* vii. 230; *SD* 229.
15. *SD* 220.
16. *SD* 224.
17. *SD* 227–28.
18. *SD* 235.
19. *SD* 248.

20. *SD* 254.
21. *SD* 325–26.
22. *Ess.* ii. 91, 93, 96.
23. *VM* ii. 134.
24. *VM* i. 189, 209.
25. *VM* ii. 422.
26. *PS* iii. 220.
27. *PS* vii. 36–38.
28. *Diff.* ii. 89.
29. *Ess.* ii. 53–54.
30. *LD* xx. 465.
31. *LD* xxvii. 139.
32. *LD* xxv. 203–4.
33. *LD* xxvii. 265.
34. *VM* i. pp. xl–xliii, xlvii–xlviii.
35. *VM* i. pp. lxvi–lxxi, lxxiv.
36. *PS* vi. 155, 156, 171.
37. *LD* xix. 129–30.
38. *Cons.* 54–55, 61.
39. *Cons.* 63, 72.
40. *Cons.* 75–76, 77, 106.
41. *Apo.* 218–20.
42. *Apo.* 224–26.
43. *Apo.* 226, 229–31.
44. *Apo.* 231–41.
45. *LD* xxv. 71.
46. *Diff.* ii. 372.
47. *LD* xxv. 71.
48. *Diff.* ii. 335, 337, 330.
49. *LD* xxv. 284.
50. *LD* xxv. 447.
51. *LD* xxvi. 35.
52. *LD* xxvii. 338.
53. *Diff.* ii. 280.
54. *Diff.* ii. 332.
55. *Diff.* ii. 320–21.
56. *Diff.* ii. 334.
57. *Diff.* ii. 307.
58. *Diff.* ii. 247–50.
59. *Diff.* ii. 252–54.

60. *Diff.* ii. 256–58.
61. *Diff.* ii. 261.
62. *VM* i. pp. xxxviii, xli, xlviii–l, lii–lvi.
63. *LD* xxv. 31–32; xxii. 99.
64. *VM* i. pp. lxxv–lxxvi.
65. *VM* i. pp. lxxx–lxxxi, lxxxvi.
66. *VM* i. pp. xciv.

6. Sacraments

1. *Apo.* 23, 29, 36–37.
2. *PS* iii. 271.
3. *PS* vi. 98.
4. *PS* viii. 57.
5. *PS* vii. 224, 226–27.
6. *LD* vi. 80.
7. *PS* iv. 63.
8. *PS* i. 274–75.
9. *PS* ii. 316.
10. *PS* iv. 342.
11. *PS* iv. 147–48.
12. *PS* vi. 136–37.
13. *PS* vi. 142–43, 146.
14. *PS* vii. 158–59.
15. *PS* v. 283.
16. *LD* xi. 129, 131, 65.
17. *LD* xi. 249–50, 232–33, 249–54.
18. *LG* 427.
19. *LD* xii. 224.
20. *PS* iv. 61.
21. *PS* iv. 304.
22. *Prepos.* 351–52.
23. *PS* viii. 165.
24. *PS* iii. 277.
25. *PS* v. 10–11.
26. *LD* v. 39.
27. *LD* v. 46–47.
28. *Jfc.* 189–90, 231, 240–41, 251, 278, 303.

29. *Jfc.* 323.
30. *Ath.* ii. 193–95.

7. Christian Life

1. *PS* i. 13, 11.
2. *PS* i. 82.
3. *PS* i. 344.
4. *PS* iv. 165.
5. *PS* vii. 100–101.
6. *PS* vii. 191.
7. *PS* viii. 242–43.
8. *PS* iv. 17.
9. *PS* i. 67, 69.
10. *PS* i. 155.
11. *PS* i. 252.
12. *PS* ii. 114.
13. *PS* viii. 29.
14. *PS* ii. 136.
15. *LD* xi. 191.
16. *PS* ii. 159.
17. *PS* iii. 217.
18. *PS* i. 68.
19. *PS* i. 95.
20. *PS* i. 167.
21. *PS* i. 142.
22. *PS* i. 145; iv. 15.
23. *PS* iii. 238.
24. *PS* iv. 5.
25. *PS* v. 242, 244, 245, 248.
26. *PS* iv. 234, 236.
27. *PS* iv. 244.
28. *PS* iv. 309–13, 317.
29. *PS* v. 109.
30. *PS* v. 340, 343.
31. *PS* vii. 198–99, 197.
32. *PS* vii. 134.
33. *PS* viii. 196–97.
34. *PS* vii. 111–13.

35. *PS* v. 53.
36. *PS* v. 69–70.
37. *PS* v. 179, 181.
38. *PS* v. 345.
39. *PS* v. 132, 254.
40. *PS* v. 210.
41. *PS* v. 220.
42. *PS* v. 343, 348, 349, 354.
43. *PS* i. 22.
44. *PS* viii. 225–27, 223.
45. *PS* iv. 4.
46. *PS* ii. 100.
47. *PS* iii. 91.
48. *PS* v. 207–8.
49. *PS* v. 193.
50. *PS* iv. 38, 96, 114, 101.
51. *PS* iv. 127–28.
52. *PS* iii. 98.
53. *PS* iii. 107.
54. *PS* iv. 105, 107–08; v. 182–84.
55. *PS* v. 241, 350.
56. *PS* v. 271, 323.
57. *PS* i. 24.
58. *PS* ii. 286, 289–90.
59. *PS* iv. 121.
60. *PS* iv. 134.
61. *PS* iv. 324.
62. *PS* iv. 337–38.
63. *PS* v. 66–67.
64. *PS* vi. 121.
65. *PS* ii. 279–80, 282.
66. *PS* i. 30.
67. *PS* i. 65.
68. *PS* v. 97.
69. *PS* v. 338.
70. *PS* vi. 322.
71. *PS* vii. 86, 84–85, 98.
72. *PS* i. 69–71.
73. *PS* iii. 210–11.
74. *PS* i. 115–17.

75. *PS* i. 102, 104.
76. *PS* i. 167.
77. *PS* i. 233.
78. *PS* iv. 15.
79. *PS* i. 252, 255.
80. *PS* i. 349.
81. *PS* i. 230, 241.
82. *PS* viii. 98.
83. *VV* 156.
84. *PS* viii. 195–96.
85. *PS* viii. 210.
86. *PS* iv. 12.
87. *PS* iv. 27.
88. *PS* iv. 29–30.
89. *PS* v. 159.
90. *PS* vi. 115.
91. *PS* iii. 80–81, 86.
92. *PS* i. 136.
93. *PS* i. 25.
94. *PS* i. 169.
95. *PS* i. 46–47.
96. *PS* i. 170.
97. *PS* i. 71.
98. *PS* ii. 272–73.
99. *PS* i. 90.
100. *PS* iv. 42.
101. *PS* v. 239.
102. *PS* vi. 186.
103. *PS* i. 30.
104. *PS* i. 172.
105. *PS* i. 70.
106. *PS* ii. 402.
107. *PS* i. 270.
108. *PS* ii. 371.
109. *PS* ii. 55.
110. *PS* v. 45.
111. *PS* i. 111.
112. *PS* i. 41–43.
113. *PS* i. 172.
114. *PS* ii. 161, 163, 171.

115. *PS* i. 232.
116. *PS* i. 73.
117. *PS* i. 51.
118. *PS* iv. 72.
119. *PS* iii. 67.
120. *PS* iv. 35.
121. *PS* iii. 295.
122. *PS* iv. 41–45.
123. *PS* vii. 10.
124. *PS* viii. 66–67.
125. *PS* v. 212–14.
126. *PS* v. 206.
127. *PS* i. 255.
128. *PS* i. 263.
129. *PS* vii. 62.
130. *PS* iv. 341.
131. *PS* v. 108.
132. *PS* ii. 161.
133. *PS* vi. 29–31.
134. *PS* vi. 189.
135. *PS* vi. 7–8.
136. *PS* vi. 35.
137. *PS* vi. 87–88, 93.
138. *PS* v. 354.
139. *PS* vi. 34.
140. *PS* vi. 43.
141. *PS* v. 107–8.
142. *PS* vi. 319.
143. *PS* viii. 141.
144. *PS* i. 324.
145. *PS* v. 226.
146. *PS* vi. 30.
147. *PS* iv. 227–28, 230–31.
148. *PS* vi. 208–9.
149. *PS* vii. 209.
150. *PS* viii. 259.
151. *PS* vi. 41–42.
152. *PS* vii. 204.
153. *PS* i. 34.
154. *PS* iv. 75.

155. *PS* i. 246, 249, 253–54.
156. *PS* i. 258, 260–64.
157. *PS* iii. 350–53, 363.
158. *PS* iii. 140, 142, 144–45, 147–48, 151.
159. *PS* vi. 22.
160. *PS* vii. 109–10.
161. *PS* v. 286.
162. *PS* v. 306–8, 310–11.
163. *PS* vi. 23.

8. Life after Death

1. *PS* iv. 216, 218–19.
2. *PS* iv. 211–12.
3. *PS* iv. 220.
4. *PS* vii. 127.
5. *PS* v. 3–4.
6. *PS* vi. 241, 247.
7. *PS* ii. 207.
8. *PS* i. 3, 5–7.
9. *PS* i. 7–8.
10. *PS* iv. 246.
11. *PS* iii. 100.
12. *PS* iv. 88.
13. *PS* i. 11.
14. *PS* i. 48–49.
15. *PS* iii. 371.
16. *PS* iii. 375–77, 382–83.
17. *Call.* 219–20.
18. GA 271–72, 323.
19. *LD* xxv. 362.
20. *VV* 350, 358–60, 366.

FURTHER READING

Newman's Writings

For details of Newman's collected and posthumous works, see the list of abbreviations before the notes. Most of the volumes in the uniform edition have been photographically reprinted by Christian Classics, Westminster, Maryland.

There are various modern paperback editions of *Apologia pro Vita Sua*, *Essay on the Development of Christian Doctrine*, *Grammar of Assent*, *Idea of a University*, *Loss and Gain*, and *Oxford University Sermons*. The eight volumes of *Parochial and Plain Sermons* have been reprinted in one volume by Ignatius Press, San Francisco (1987).

Ian Ker's *The Genius of John Henry Newman: Selections from his Writings* (Oxford: Clarendon Press, 1989) is a comprehensive anthology. Joyce Sugg has anthologized the letters in *A Packet of Letters* (Oxford: Clarendon Press, 1983).

Secondary Works

C. S. Dessain's *John Henry Newman* (London: Nelson, 1966) is the best introduction to Newman's thought. Dessain's *The Spirituality of John Henry Newman* (Minneapolis: Winston Press, 1977), also published as *Newman's Spiritual Themes* (Dublin: Veritas Publications, 1977), is a good introduction to the spirituality of Newman. See also Hilda Graef, *God and Myself: The Spirituality of John Henry Newman* (London: P. Davies, 1967). W. D. White's *The Preaching of John Henry Newman*

179

(Philadelphia: Fortress Press, 1969) contains a useful selection of the sermons, together with an introductory essay on Newman's preaching. Ian Ker's *John Henry Newman: A Biography* (Oxford: Clarendon Press, 1988) includes discussions and summaries of all the theological writings. Ker's *The Achievement of John Henry Newman* (Notre Dame, Ind.: University of Notre Dame Press, 1990) examines, among other topics, Newman's impressive contributions as a preacher and a theologian.

INDEX

Alexandrian Church: Christology, 40–41; economy, 22–23; revelation and paganism, 17–18; sacraments, 107. *See also* Early Church; Fathers of the Church

Ambrose: role as bishop, 86

Anglican Church: *See* Church of England

Antecedent judgment: faith and evidence, 6

Antecedent probability: doctrinal development, 34–35; role in faith, 1–8

Apologia pro Vita Sua, 107; Alexandrian Church, paganism, and revelation, 17–18; probability and certitude, 8–9

Apostles: holy nature of, 127

Aquinas, Thomas: Mary's sinfulness, 68; sin and incarnation, 41

Argument: faith and reason, 4–5, 7

Arian heresy: laity's faithfulness, 86

The Arians of the Fourth Century: atonement, emphasis on crucifixion, 43; dogma, 26; dogma and revelation, 22; early Church, 17–18

Ascension: redemption, 49–50

Assumption of Mary, 62, 64–65, 68–69

Athanasius, 102; Christology, 40; foundation of Mariology, 65; role as bishop, 86

Atonement: chief doctrine of Gospels, 39; crucifixion, attention paid to, 43

"Attendance on Holy Communion," 111–12

Augustine, 86, 94

Authority: dispensation and doctrinal development, 36; Scripture's authority and doctrinal development, 35

Baptism, 108–9; holiness, obligation to, 120; initiation, 109–10. *See also* Sacraments

Beliefs: actions consistent with, 141

Bossuet, Jacques Bénigne: doctrinal development, 32

Butler, Joseph: *The Analogy of Religion*, 8, 107

Callista, 20, 159

Calmness: mark of a mature Christian, 145–46; prayer, 149–50

Chalcedon, Council of, 100

Christian life: asceticism, 145–52; changing one's nature, 127; cheerful aspects of repentance, 133; consistency, 139–41; conversion, 129–30; cooperation with grace necessary for holiness, 128; daily self-denial, 123, 135–36; fasting, 146–47; feelings and actions, 141; formal prayer, 150–51; free will, 128; Gospels as burden and joy,